Catherine of Siena

Essays on
Her Life and Thought

**Edited with an Introduction and Notes by
Thomas McDermott, O.P.**

NEW PRIORY PRESS

EXPLORING THE DOMINICAN VISION

i

Contents

CATHERINE OF SIENA – ESSAYS

Editor's Preface

This volume is a collection of essays on the life and thought of St. Catherine of Siena (1347-80), a Dominican *mantellata* or penitential woman who was declared a Doctor of the Church by Pope Paul VI in 1970. Several of the articles were written years ago but were never translated into English and/or published until now. All of them have been selected on the basis of making a significant contribution to Catherinian studies.

Chapter 1, "Theology in the Life of St. Catherine of Siena" by Thomas Deman, O.P., is one of the most important essays on her thought of the 20th century. This is a translation of "La théologie dans la vie de sainte Catherine de Sienne" in *Supplément à la "Vie Spirituelle* (1 Janvier 1935): pp. 1-24, by Dr. Pauline Nugent, C.C.V.I., Ph.D., of the Department of Modern and Classical Languages, Missouri State University, Springfield, Missouri, U.S.A. A slightly different version of this article was published in Italian as "La teologia nella vita di S. Caterina da Siena" in *Studi cateriniani* XI (1935), pp. 45-56. Thomas Deman (1899-1955) was a noted Dominican moral theologian.

Chapter 2, "Catherine of Siena: Doctor of Communion" by Thomas McDermott, O.P., originally appeared in *Il servizio dottrinale di Caterina da Siena,* volume 4 in the series *Quaderni del Centro Internazionale di Studi Cateriniani* (Firenze, 2012), pp. 53-78. In the article I attempt to show how Catherine's ever increasing communion with the Trinity is reflected in her growing fraternal communion with her neighbor. I go on to identify the characteristics of her human relationships and her impact on others. I also take a look at her theological methodology, way of "doing" theology, and relevance today.

In Chapter 3, "Freedom and Politics in St. Catherine of Siena," Maria Francesca Carnea examines Catherine's involvement in the political affairs of fourteenth century Italy and her motives. This work of careful scholarship by Dr. Carnea, an Italian researcher and expert on St. Catherine, originally appeared in Italian in four parts in the periodical *Ave Maria* published by the Dominican Sisters of St. Catherine of Siena, Nursing and Teaching, Rome. The article was subsequently translated into English by Sister Marialuisa Buratti, O.P., and appeared in the

English edition of the same journal in 2011. The notes were translated by myself.

Chapter 4, "The Holy Spirit in the Prayers of St. Catherine of Siena," is written by Yves Congar, O.P. (1904-95), the renowned French Dominican theologian who has been described as the single most formative influence on the Second Vatican Council. This is a translation of "Le Saint-Esprit dans les prières de Sainte Catherine de Sienne" which appeared in *Atti del Congresso Internazionale di Studi Cateriniani, Siena-Roma, 24-26 aprile 1980* (Roma: Curia Generalizia O.P., 1981), pp. 333-337. The original French version is available online. This first-ever English translation was done by Dr. Pauline Nugent, C.C.V.I. (see above).

In Chapter 5, Fr. Michael J. Houser of L'Istituto Patristico Augustini-anum, Rome, presents the first English translation of one of the most important primary sources of Catherine's life: a major portion of the deposition of Dominican Friar Bartolomeo Dominici (1343-1415), one of her closest disciples. This translation of the original Latin text is part of the collection of testimonies of twenty-four witnesses known as the *Processo Castellano* for the eventual canonization process in Venice which was begun forty-two years after her death in 1380. Dominici was introduced to Catherine by his fellow Dominican novice Tommaso della Fonte, a relative of hers. He became a lifelong friend and disciple and accompanied her to Pisa, Lucca, and Avignon. After her death he became active in the reform of the Order as Prior Provincial of the Roman Province and Procurator General of the Order. This is a translation of most of the second part of Dominici's testimony in which he responds to the defects or difficulties of his first deposition where it appeared to contradict Raymond of Capua's *Legenda maior* or biography of Catherine. The original text is found in *Fontes vitae S. Catharinae Senensis historici: Il processo castellano*, volume 9, edited by Marie H. Laurent (1942), pp. 324-344. The opening paragraph is from page 1 of the introduction to the *Processo* in the Laurent edition.

Chapter 6, "The Spiritual Life in the Teaching of St. Catherine of Siena" by Antoine Lemonnyer, O.P., is the most significant essay in this collection. Published originally in 1932 by the French Dominicans under the title *Notre vie spirituelle à l'école de Sainte Catherine de Sienne,* it was reprinted by Cerf in 2009. The author's systematic and careful study of Catherine's teaching on the virtues, part of the core of her spiritual thought, is very important in the study of medieval spirituality.This translation, published here for the first time, is the work of the late Sister Mary of the Trinity, O.P., of Corpus Christi Monastery, Menlo Park, California.

Antonin Lemonnyer (1872-1932) was a theologian of the first rank who taught for many years at *Le Saulchoir* ("the place planted with willows"), a former Cistercian abbey in Kain, Belgium, that was the *studium generale* of the Province of France following the expulsion of religious in 1903. The influence of *Le Saulchoir* at the Second Vatican Council is well known especially through the work of Marie-Dominique Chenu, O.P., and Yves Congar, O.P.

Lemonnyer shared the radical view of other well-known Dominican theologians Juan-Gonzalez Arintero (†1928), Ambroise Gardeil (†1931), one of the original organizers of *Le Saulchoir*, and Reginald Garrigou-Lagrange (†1964) that all the baptized are called to mystical contemplation. This view, which the Church gave explicit expression to at the Second Vatican Council in "the universal call to holiness" (see "Lumen Gentium," Chapter V) was *contra* the more traditional opinions of the Jesuits and Carmelites. He is also noted for having worked strenuously against the separation of moral theology and spiritual theology. In 1907 he founded, with A.M. Jacquin, the *Revue des sciences philosophiques et théologiques* which is still in existence. After serving as Regent of Studies for his province, he went on to become assistant for the intellectual life to the Master of the Order, Martin Gillet. Anyone wanting to study St. Catherine of Siena's spirituality, particularly as it pertains to the virtues, will find Lemonnyer's work invaluable.

For an introduction to Catherine's thought, I refer readers to my *Catherine of Siena: Spiritual development in her life and teaching* (Paulist, 2008), and *Catherine of Siena: Doctor of the Church* by Giacinto D'Urso, O.P. (New Priory Press, 2013).

It is my hope that this volume will further the study of Catherine of Siena's mystical thought. I am grateful to the contributors to this volume as well as to Albert Judy, O.P., of New Priory Press, for assisting in its publication.

Thomas McDermott, O.P.
Regent of Studies
Central Province, U.S.A.
Solemnity of St. Joseph, 2015

1

Theology in the Life of St. Catherine of Siena

Thomas Deman, O.P.

We have several approaches at our disposal to get to know St. Catherine and to penetrate just a little into the secret of her soul. We may study her style and language which are a faithful expression of her personality; we may observe the influence she exercises on her epoch and define her historical role; or we may tackle her spiritual life itself directly and audaciously. You will indulge a theologian's choice to pursue the third method. For one who professes to study God and the things of God it should not be totally impossible to have some awareness of how God invades a holy soul. No other object of study is more beautiful nor more passionate, even if such an undertaking is difficult.

♔

From the first contact with St. Catherine one is surprised at how intellectual this woman is. A thousand matters entreat her assistance and absorb her attention: she applies herself wholeheartedly in the face of so much misery; she carries on her shoulders the burden of the universal Church; and still she devoted serious attention to thought. That she dictated a considerable number of letters is not only the sign of an admirable profusion of eloquence—the privilege of the Tuscan race— but it is also proof of a remarkable aptitude in handling ideas and reflection. Toward the end of her life she wrote a book—her own book—which she apparently valued greatly. She spoke of it to her correspondents and recommended it to the care of Raymond of Capua in the letter of February 15, 1380. It is a sort of last will and testament, a work, which will eventually be called her Dialogue--the book of divine doctrine.[1] She gives this book a remarkable intellectual character, and not simply supplies thoughts for edification and exhortation.

This first impression withstands a more attentive examination, to the point that the theologian soon discovers a relationship between his own spirit and that of Catherine. Granted, she uses imagination and allegory more than he himself does. (Does she not have the right to be a poet and to remain a woman?). Granted her discourse enjoys a liberty and profusion that the works of theology certainly do not permit. (But shall we impose on this saint the methodology of a professor?). It only remains to say that the subjects which she treats and the themes she develops are those of theology; and one finds in her writings the questions, distinctions, indeed even certain technical terms that this science employs. If one or other of her theories are of Augustinian origin, such as the division of the human soul into memory, intellect, and will, seen as image of the Trinity, she also writes pages on the Beatitudes that are rigorously and specifically Thomistic. Here we do not find original or curious concepts, but thoughts that meet the test of the most classical theology; it is in this that the intellect of St. Catherine clearly takes delight. In this sense she brings into play precise and defined ideas, and even if she says only one word in passing, we sense that it comes from an informed spirit. We experience an intellectual satisfaction in reading this mystic. Moreover, her ideas are solid, constant and firm, securely planted in her spirit to the point that they constitute a type of system of which she sometimes gives a more complete exposition according to the occasion (cf. Letters 48, 51, etc.).[2] But we must be careful that her resoluteness is not taken for rigidity: faithful to what she is thinking, she adapts the expression to the needs or capacities of her audience. She says the same thing, but she says it differently, depending on whether she is writing to a Jew, a princess, a grieving mother, a religious: she possesses a gift of versatility and mobility, which is nothing else than a refined understanding of concrete situations and the consciousness of what is original in each particular case. And this is a quality of spirit that

---

[1] This letter is in two parts, Letters 371 and 373, and is the last of Catherine's extant correspondence. (Ed.)

[2] The numbering system of Catherine's letters by N. Tommaseo is followed. For a complete edition of the letters, see *Le lettere di S. Caterina da Siena*, 6 vols, ed. P. Misciattelli, 1939. English translation: *The Letters of Catherine of Siena*, 4 vols, trans. and ed. Suzanne Noffke, OP, 2000-2008. (Ed.)

theologians at least recommend in their lectures, even if they do not always give an incontestable example of it in practice.

This rapport is even more pronounced when we discover in this woman a sense of order and of the respective value of things (a quality eminently intellectual and theological). Such a quality can be seen in her famous Letter 213 on discretion, and in her repeated teachings on penance as a means and not an end. Catherine even conceptualizes a grandiose view of the hierarchical universe, where each creature in its rank glorifies God, and where people are providentially linked one to another by bonds of charity. She marvels at the human being and his soul which is so well adapted to love God: here she surrenders herself— a rare faculty with her—and trembles before the invisible. She discerns infallibly the essential from the accidental and entertains an exclusive preference for rigorous thought which admirably enshrine the formulae of Niccolò Tommaseo: "Out of love she identifies with all creatures. ... This pure soul rejoices in every form of good, and picks only the flower."

Catherine's temperament, vigorously realistic with love and admiration for all that is created and that comes from the hands of God, perdures even under the pain and sadness of the sins which these goods cause us to commit. She writes these admirable words: "It is not the prestige and delights of the world nor the creatures that are reprehensible, but only the affection that the person invests in them...." (Letter 29). Moreover, this woman of fiery temperament passes perfectly balanced judgments on people and on things such that one would think they were conceived at the desk of a moral theologian when instead they have burst forth alive from her soul. She knows the value that works done in the state of sin can retain and the recompense they can merit; the inviolable dignity that still belongs to fallen priests; and that one can do good in whatever condition he finds himself, even if he is not a friar. With respect to sinners, she mingles rigor and compassion in just and happy proportions. Even when she is swept up in the most profound way, the many subordinate clauses in her sentences attest that she does not lose the lucidity and justice of her spirit. Will you forgive me if, having observed these various traits of intellect and of Catherine's thought, I considered them characteristics of the theological spirit and allow me to see a relationship between this saint and the theologian?

⚜

But then a problem becomes inevitable. I do not at all wish to mention the problem of the origin of Catherine's theological thought because the solution, at least in general terms, is immediately apparent. It is clear that this woman was naturally endowed with superior intellect (sharpness, penetration, certainty, vigor were its complementary qualities) and that she learned excellent religious teaching her whole life long. But it is no less certain that her thought, apart from human teaching and natural reflection, felt the aftereffects of a privileged contact with God, the Father of lights. Our problem is certainly not there. Instead, it would be better rather to investigate the relation between Catherine's thought and life.

For if it is true that she excels in knowledge, as we have briefly stated, it is no less true that her life did not consist purely in knowledge. Catherine was creative, and her life is evidence of this. Assuming that her thought was of eminent theological quality, there would be nothing paradoxical in seeing in her a learned woman for whom ideas are the reason for living. She has within herself an indomitable power which soon makes her leave her cell and her home to go out in the world and bring God to it. She mingles with her century, whose soul she would want to become. She teaches her confessors, she directs her mother, she reprimands or exhorts priests, she negotiates with republics, and with all of her commanding and inflexible will she spurs on "Christ on earth," the Pope. But she would not have had this audacity and it would not have succeeded for her, if she had not first of all accomplished a great work in herself and cultivated a great love. Catherine is power, Catherine is will, Catherine is fire. She commands, she dominates, she subdues. It is scarcely possible at this point to verify accurately M. Bergson's idea of the great mystics.[3] But in such a life, what is the place of thought since thought in Catherine is so remarkable? In this sanctity and in this apostolate, what is the role of theology—since Catherine's thought is eminently theological? The investigation that we would like to undertake on the spiritual life of our saint becomes clear in this problem, and its terms, so to speak, have been dictated to us by Catherine herself.

---

[3] Henri Bergson, in *Les Deux Sources de la morale et de la religion* (1932), opposes mysticism to doctrine. (Ed.)

To inquire about the spiritual life of such a soul is tantamount to asking if the best of Catherine was not this creative and loving power which we have just mentioned, so that thought played only an accidental and secondary role; or perhaps thought was not wholly one, so to speak, with this power, and did not pertain at all to this creative energy itself such that the life of Catherine was imbued with knowledge and with truth. According as we must choose one or other of these solutions, the personality of Catherine and the nature of the mystical life in general will appear to us to be noticeably different. We shall see our saint as the prey of what M. Bergson calls an emotion, and theology will only be slightly present. Or perhaps her life will present itself as the realization of a truth: the incarnation, should we say, of a true doctrine, in an exceptionally powerful being; and Catherine will pour forth God because she is undoubtedly possessed of him, in her intellect no less than in her will. In this last case we would have the right to judge that the mystic life, and that means human life in the highest expression that Christianity gives it, is objective knowledge as well as interior emotion; that the concern for truth in action, far from hindering the momentum, provokes it and gives it this soundness in vigor, which is the sign and the honor of the most beautiful human lives.

We may search for the solution of the problem thus posed in the teachings of Catherine. We are naturally inclined to think that these teachings, especially if they are repeated, constant and systematic, translate the experience peculiar to the person who propagates them. If our saint is concerned with the relationship of thought to life, of theology to the Christian life, we shall learn from this, it seems, what she practiced. But it is striking how she attributes an important role to knowledge, to light, and to truth in the renouncing of sin and the acquiring of virtue, to the point that this trait is one of the most original in her letters—to which we are restricting this first attempt at a solution for the reason that will be stated shortly.

Because she is not content to merely counsel but intends to lead her correspondents to virtue, Catherine goes so far as to show them the paths by which they will acquire it. But what does she point out? We would expect well-regulated exercises of the will, a progressive asceticism that gradually habituates the will and rebellious characters to the good. There is none of this. Catherine invites us to knowledge. She understands that by the ways of knowledge and of truth, one would arrive at an effective practice of good. We would consider these two

5

very different categories: the one is knowledge, the other action. But Catherine no doubt appreciates that there is a connection from one to the other. It is on these terms that she exhorts to patience, a virtue of energy like no other; and all her care is to point out to her correspondent, the merchant Marco Bindi, what is the precise knowledge he will need to acquire this virtue: God is, and all that is comes from God. God is goodness, he wishes only our good, our tribulations are the work of his love, our sins have deserved that God punish us. These are not researched considerations, we note, but some elementary truths of faith chosen with a view to obtaining from the soul the virtuous reaction which they seem to call forth by their nature, and expressed on Catherine's part with all the vehemence of her own conviction (Letter 13). She adopts the same method when it comes to humility, that profound attitude of the heart, saying that it is the sole means of acquiring self-knowledge—something she says repeatedly. Above all, Catherine taught the same about love, and since the perfection of all the virtues is tied to the perfection of love, her doctrine here takes a universal scope that invites us to view her a little more closely.

Catherine is very firm on this point—as on all others. As a general principle, for her there is the truth that God loves us. One discovers it in God's works, which he made for us: Creation, the Incarnation, the Blood of the Lamb--the blood where Catherine reads, as in an open book, the most beautiful secrets of the heart of God. But we also see this truth in ourselves, since the one who knows himself knows that he is nothing and that he receives from God all that he is. What matters is this knowledge. That is the decisive turning point, as also the risks and the difficulties, for it happens that people do not know this first and fundamental truth. It is not that we are incapable of learning it: Catherine teaches that every reasoning creature carries within himself a natural light, the discernment of good and evil, such that if one does not allow it to become obscured, but exercises it in the pursuit of good and the flight from evil, one soon acquires a more powerful supernatural light. However, with certain people self-love is precisely a cloud, and all evil derives from the fact that our lights have been obfuscated. Where the light reigns, one could say that things work automatically and that love appears the most natural thing in the world. Is it not indeed a type of love that the light shows us? Is not the truth the fact that God loves us? Now, man is so made that he is moved to see himself loved, and that he soon loves in return the one who first loved him. It is thus that the love of God is born in the heart of man: "With the light we acquire love from love" (Letter 304). What Catherine says here connects with what she teaches elsewhere about the succession of the powers of the soul, where the intellect along with the memory is set in motion and incites love. As for the cloud of self-love (and Catherine includes under this word, in accordance with the usage of theology, the sum of our unregulated attachments), it is certain that one does not dispel it except by painful effort, with hatred of self, says Catherine energetically, and one recovers in this way his place in the process of affective asceticism. We could not expect that Catherine would dispense us from this. But what remains characteristic is that when self-love is dispelled, the soul returns to the light which then does its own work and produces virtue.

Charity, sprung from light, is mother of all the virtues which she engenders alive. Therefore, there is a dependence of these virtues—in other words, of the entire spiritual life—on the light. Let us listen to our saint: "And if I consider it carefully, no other virtue has life in itself if it is not formed and exercised in the soul with this light of truth" (Letter 227). And in this way our activities themselves, our good works, become an irradiation of the light. We then understand Catherine's exclamations:

> O truth, ancient and new, the soul who possesses you is freed from the poverty of darkness and has the riches of light. By light, I do not at all mean mental visions nor other consolations, but the light of truth; and that means that by knowing the truth in the blood, the soul is drunk, tasting God through love of charity with the light of most holy faith. It is with that faith that all our works ought to be seasoned, as we rejoice to eat the food of souls for the honor of God on the table of the most holy Cross.... From where does the soul inherit this desire? From truth. How has she seen and known it? With the light of faith. And on what has her glance fallen so as to see it? On the blood of the Crucified Christ. In what vessel has she found it? In herself when she knew herself...." (Letter 227)

We see that M. Bergson is correct in one sense in saying that mystics do not attach great importance to their ecstasies—preparatory phenomena, incidents along the way—nevertheless, they are far from being indifferent to truth since they admit to drawing their action and enthusiasm from it. The distinction of Catherine, "light of mental visions, light of truth", definitely corrects the assessment of the French philosopher.

Catherine offers the teaching that we have just recalled to anyone who would understand it: to sinners who have succumbed because they had lost the light and who raise themselves up again once they recover it; to religious of every habit and therefore of every spirituality—not only to Friars Preachers; to women, and to the unlearned like the spouse of Bernabò Visconti, like Catherine's mother, Lapa, who was the wife of a dyer: "You ought with a true and holy solicitude apply yourself to know that you are not and to recognize your being as coming from God" (Letter 1). The method is universal. And the result of this is that the variation in the virtues—their diminution or growth—depends, as Catherine herself says, on the variation of light.

Will this method seem to us optimistic and naïve? There are, however, reasons to think that it was not ineffectual. To understand this, let us note that the saint exhorts her correspondents to know God and to know themselves—which is not the same thing as to furnish them with ready-made knowledge—which leaves its imprint on their spirit like the image on a photographic plate. She means that everyone should be convinced of the love of God and of one's own misery which would require, it seems, a great purity of heart and assiduous meditation. Such knowledge is like a fruit whose flavor she could taste but which first required a slow maturation to attain that flavor. It comes from the depths of the spirit where it is formed; it is like an expression of the soul. How different it is from the superficial phenomenon which people sometimes designate by the word knowledge! But when the truth is thus known there naturally ensues in the soul a movement toward good. And this trait is one of the most significant of Catherine's psychology. According to the opinion most in vogue today, what requires explanation is that man does good; according to Catherine, we must explain how it is he comes to do evil. It is there we seek the causes of good because we think that man naturally inclines rather toward evil. Here, persuaded that in his essence and at the root of his moral life, man wills the good, one now seeks the causes of evil. Hence Catherine's famous teaching on self-love, principle of the deviation of a natural tendency. In fact, she will say that self-love makes us look for the good where it is not, not that it inclines us toward evil. When the obstacle is removed, nature runs its course. And provided that one recognizes the good, one will naturally love it. Catherine explained this in a text which could have been written by a philosopher who was most meticulous in his use of words: "By its very nature, the soul always desires the good and good things; but its error consists in this: the darkness of self-love, having removed the light, causes it to look for the good where it is not to be found" (Letter 301). Therein lies the secret of the efficacy we seek: a method that exhorts us above all else to knowledge. It is only by beginning from this point of departure, if we may say so, that the soul follows its proper course. It is so constituted that it is then borne along toward virtue. If it is true that we have unfortunately a thousand means of evading the dictates of the spirit (and it is about this that we are thinking when we claim that knowledge is essentially ineffectual), it is still more true (for we are now passing from the accidental, however multiform it may be, to the natural), that from this knowledge we fall prey to seduction that anticipates, so to speak, the fundamental desire of the will. The human being is sensitive to truth even in the depths of his heart. Moreover, it appears nowhere in Catherine's teaching that we approach the good independently of knowledge or that the will bears within itself its own immanent and infallible direction. She does not ignore what a soul may owe to love, and what happy influence love may exert over knowledge itself as, for example, charity over faith. But she never holds that love is self-sufficient.

We now arrive at this answer: that the efficacy of the soul, according to Catherine's method, comes from its very makeup. But, how might one obtain from the soul the hoped for reactions if there were not such truths as are capable of determining these good sentiments? Before everything else, there is the truth that God loves us, with all the other truths that are related to it. This is a fact. And it is because she can propose to souls such an object of true knowledge that Catherine has secured from them the love of God and the practice of virtue.

In short, her art was to take account of what is, of the admirable magnificence of what is, while so many others, who pretend also to convert, act as if the soul must draw everything from its own depth, without any prior action on God's part. And this time we must respond that the efficacy of Catherine's method merges with the power of reality on the entire soul.

Someone may lodge an objection against this first investigation which we have just completed. We might say that in all her teachings, Catherine aims to lead toward the good men or women who do not possess her own gifts. Her method, therefore, is intended for the use of average souls. Catherine herself does not go through the paths of understanding. She makes use of an emotion incomparably more powerful than reasoning or thought. And if we want to reconstruct the personal experience of Catherine we must, therefore, try to describe a force and a creative fervor, not an academic concern. We do not believe that this line of argument would be decisive, but rather than argue the point we have recourse to unimpeachable witnesses. The *Spiritual Document* spells out the method Catherine used for her own sanctification, and it is striking that knowledge is there held in honor, just as in the letters.[4] But the *Dialogue* ought especially to teach us by unmasking for us, as seen in her own experience, the way in which her thought was in communication with her creative power.

Let us first recall briefly that the *Dialogue*, which has a pronounced doctrinal and didactic character, as we said above, is a response to the great desires in the soul of Catherine and seems to constitute the development of that exceptional emotion which she shared with Raymond of Capua in that famous letter (272). Throughout its composition, the book is, as it were, interspersed with the interventions and reactions of Catherine, who gives thanks, who prays, who expresses her happiness and her afflictions. So then, it is a book of doctrine, but one whose link with the vibrant soul of Catherine is not unrecognizable. It is not like the work of a thinker whose life is scarcely engaged in his thoughts. Our concern will be first to examine the connection thus outlined. We are not advancing anything unverifiable, rather drawing attention to a rigorous conformity between the truths that this book establishes and the practical attitudes expressed in the life of Catherine in so far as it contains the most personal details. There is nothing superfluous in this book. Many pages have the character of pure doctrinal expositions, apparently raising theological speculation; others are simply descriptions of customs, with a precision and a piercing energy. Indeed, it is not hard to notice the interest that each and every

---

[4] The critical text by R. Fawtier is in the collection *Catheriniana* (excerpt from *Mélanges d'Archéologie et d'Histoire* published by l'Ecole Française de Rome, vol. XXXIV (1914), pp. 86-93. (Deman). The *Spiritual Document,* a summary of Catherine's spiritual teaching, was dictated by her to the Augustinian hermit William of Flete when she visited him at Lecceto on January 7, 1377. For an English translation, see Benedict Hackett, OSA, *William Flete, OSA, and Catherine of Siena. Masters of fourteenth century spirituality.* Villanova, PA: Augustinian Press, 1992, pp. 183-184; Augusta Theodosia Drane, *The History of St. Catherine of Siena and Her Companions,* 4th Ed., 2 vols. London: Longman, 1915, vol. II, pp. 359-362. (Ed.)

person has in the specific life of our saint. Catherine speaks at great length about God. But what does she consider? His love, his gifts, his providence. She is certainly not concerned with his hidden mysteries and interior being, but rather his relationship with created things and with humankind. Once she was giving advice about this to one of her correspondents: "...wishing to penetrate not the secret things of God in His hidden mysteries, but only his will and the sweetness of his charity which loved us so inestimably, and seeks and wants nothing else but our sanctification" (Letter 48). The *Dialogue* complies with the same thought. But it is clear that such knowledge of God demands and confirms a certain attitude of confidence, abandonment, and love—which is precisely one of Catherine's most urgent recommendations. Nothing is so beautiful as this inviolable peace and joy experienced by the perfect soul in the midst of tribulations. This is a spirituality sweet and profound, whose link with God, as we have described Him, is manifest. The *Dialogue* also speaks much about sinners, either recounting their sins or analyzing their fall and condition. But, it is there that sin is for Catherine, at the same time, a subject of both horror and of compassion—sentiments corresponding precisely to a certain knowledge that she has of sin, in conformity with the doctrine of faith and theology. And she moves naturally from that realization to the desire to expiate sin.

But the place allotted to the neighbor in Catherine's considerations is especially remarkable. Love and service of neighbor are considered the characteristic signs of perfection. To justify this thought, all sorts of arguments are brought into play. By following the correct paths, these lead to the original idea of a perfection deriving from the strength of the soul and from patience rather than from contemplation. We might say that with Catherine the sense of the honor and glory of God triumphs over the desire to take her rest in the interior beauty of God. Perfect souls on earth are happy people, but so are also those who suffer. And in heaven itself, the elect, united to God in the vision of his essence, will feast on the glory of God accomplished in everything. In the same sense, the apostolate, as seen in the *Dialogue,* becomes the object of a real theology which formulates its laws and justifies its exercise notably in the form of desire and expiation. The sense of charity triumphs over external works even as the infinite does over the finite. There is redemption in suffering and the neighbor is as concerned with our sins as with our virtues. It is in this regard that the link between doctrine and life appears in all its force in the author of the *Dialogue.* Theological considerations seem to flow into an increasing desire for the salvation of souls. To the extent that she is better informed of these matters, Catherine also feels more oppressed with the need to suffer and to weep so that God may grant mercy. Here we are witnessing the drama of Catherine's apostolic vocation. In a word, she deals of nothing but this concept throughout the entire *Dialogue*. This book does not answer abstract questions; it responds to the torment of a soul. And her torment is to throw herself into the fray and to wrench from God, with groans and tears and blood, the salvation of sinners and of the Church. The doctrines that the book sets in play converge toward this attitude and culminate there. These are theological pages, but ones that recount the history of a soul. And it is the very holiness of Catherine, her holiness of power and conquest that seems to mature throughout these thoughts.

It remains for us to interpret the connection between doctrine and Catherine's life which will be established from now on. Shall we maintain that the holiness of Catherine derives strictly from her learning and that it is a response in her life to the theological concepts that were first present in her mind? It is not totally impossible that this is the situation. But, as for the present case, it is clear that the theological themes of the *Dialogue* represent a choice and that their grouping is controlled by an exigency other than pure logic. When Catherine elaborates them, she has already possessed her desire and she concludes learnedly that it is necessary to suffer for the salvation of souls and has put the will for expiation at the basis of her reasoning. Thus we may explain the originality of the conclusions of the *Dialogue.* It would be good to verify if this idea of perfection as the service of neighbor in his suffering, if the orientation of all interior progress toward this overflow of love of neighbor, is not a great innovation for its time, and if, in the history of spirituality, Catherine did not give expression to something that until then had not been deduced from theology. We do not then deny, in Catherine's case, a psychological priority of emotion over distinct knowledge. But, in our opinion, this is not the decisive point. That seems to us to lie in the exquisite correlation between emotion and thought. We cannot dispute that Catherine does her best in a passionate manner. We cannot dispute that she takes extreme care to discover the doctrinal laws of her practical expression. Most certainly, she is driven and she will yield; but not blindly. Someone might say that she has only an intellectual need to enunciate the theory of one's actions, and to reduce to an abstract formula the rules of her own conduct, without the need for action to receive any real extraneous influence. But if we must admit, as we did at first, that the theological themes are here chosen and arranged in harmony with the disposition of a particular soul, we must also acknowledge that the object of our search is not a doctrine that is gently tilted toward our need to justify what we have already decided to establish. The doctrine is pure and intact. Detached from the vital context where it is introduced, it would still preserve its value. Is not the skillfulness of Catherine in fact quite extraordinary? Let us note again that the passages in the *Dialogue* are legion where God concludes his sharing by formulas like the following: I have taught you these things so that you may atone for the salvation of souls. Let us re-read a few lines from the conclusion of the entire work:

> [Catherine says to the eternal Father:] In the light of faith, I am strong, constant and persevering. In the light of faith, I hope; it will not let me falter on the way. This light teaches me the way; and without this light I would go into the darkness. And this is why I said to you, Eternal Father, that you indeed wish to illuminate me in the light of the most holy faith.... O Trinity eternal, in your light which you have given me, and receiving it with the light of the most holy faith, I have known, by many admirable explanations, smoothing out for me the path of great perfection, that I ought to serve you with light and not with darkness, to be a mirror of a good and holy life, to lift myself out of my miserable life, where always through my insufficiency, I have served you in the darkness. I did not know your Truth and that is why I did not love it.... (*Dialogue,* chapter 167)

Why not yield to the suggestions which these texts and remarks evoke? They invite us to consider that knowledge for Catherine has an interest with regard to her own actions. Everything happens as if she intends to exercise control over her own emotions and not allow herself to be carried away unless she is sure. Nothing is so moving for us as a St. Catherine determined to verify the magnificent impulse that lifts her up. Did she not have reason to be undisturbed? Did she not experience in the very love that burned within her a sort of simple and irresistible persuasion? If it happens that we are convinced of the value of certain cries that seem to arise from the better depths of ourselves, how could this incomparable soul not also have been invaded with the power of God? And yet she accurately reflects at length and in a doctrinal way on her action because she is anxious about its truth. Of course, one regards the action of mystics as admirable when it is presented as their own creation. But without doubt we diminish the scope of their thought when we render it as a simple translation of their emotion, as if the notes of a symphony, jumping off the page, could accurately translate the original and ineffable inspirations of the composer. There is in their very creation a requirement of correctness to that which satisfies the intervention of thought. In this sense, it is not a pure creation. But the action of the mystic consists in the conformity to an objective rule of which thought is the authentic interpretation. Just as God created, not in a single stroke of his power alone, but "in weight, number and measure", according to the idea he has of things, so the mystic, this collaborator of God, intends to move only in respect to what is, subject to the laws that define the nature of things and to the thought of God. This is why we were saying that the mystic expects his action to be in conformity with truth. It is possible that an emotion is not always attached to an object and that sensitivity has its own inventiveness which depends only on itself. It would even be possible that certain moral inventions, for example, the idea of justice as the inviolable dignity of the human person, might have come from faculties other than reason. But with mystics, the union of emotion and action with thought occurs infallibly. Having come to this passionate and pure point, the love of the good is, so to speak, penetrated with an ardent need of truth; and when the mystic yields, it is because he is sure, in his intellect, that he is not mistaken. We are not saying that this concept does not entail inconveniences in a philosophy that downgrades intellect; but it seems to us by far the most authentic witness to what St. Catherine has revealed about herself.

It also seems that Catherine draws power for her actions from what she knows. She says so and she demonstrates it. But is there power for action in thought? From the most widespread opinions in vogue and even going so far as the penetrating analysis of M. Bergson, it seems that everything today conspires against this claim. Sterility, vanity, the impotence of knowing! Thought would be by definition something detached from life, and action is not an issue, having its own demands and resources whether ignoramuses accomplish magnificent exploits under some inspiration or other, and the learned offer the spectacle of an ironic contradiction between their lives and their theories. But shall we obliterate the example of a St. Catherine? It is better to admit that human intellect is not always inefficient speculation. Intellect is able to present itself in relationship to an object such that the conduct or aspect of life finds itself changed. One only needs to acknowledge with all possible rigor and impartiality the source of the speculative appearance of this knowledge. But knowledge has power over life. Why would there not be objects whose seduction carries us along? The good always moves us; it is only a matter of discovering it. Basically, would not the secret of sanctity and of the high moral life be here in the discovery of the good that seduces us in a holy manner? And if that sanctity is so rare, does not its final cause also lie in the mediocre functioning of the intellect that is fixed on banal objects and too lazy to look up to higher matters? It could be that the work of our sanctification ought to begin with purification and be maintained by the elevation of the spirit. We profess a radical docility of the will to the role of the intellect. Not that other forces do not solicit this power nor that the will never digresses outside the ways of true judgment. But when the will is true to its nature, it obeys. It is not that the will does not forewarn our judgment with its presentiments; judgment requires it. Knowledge is certainly not a pure theoretic function; it is also endowed with practical application. Intellect likewise issues a judgment about it which is much more than a correct statement of the action to be done; it is a command that it promulgates authoritatively so that a person lives by it. Intellect, teacher of life; powerful knowledge of action; theology, the principle of holiness; these are the formulae that one must believe with one's whole heart. And we understand that the more the desire to do good increases in a person, the more also one falls in love with rectitude and yields authority to his intellect. From the clear knowledge of the good, he derives a force which goes as far as enthusiasm. Pure doctrine becomes moving for him. Is this not a complete picture of our saint? From thoughts about theology and faith she deduces judgments that are charged with energy, and capable of penetrating to the core of the soul, insinuating themselves into her powers of implementation, and swelling, if I may say so, the sails that must carry her toward the realm of the good!

We shall better express the efficacy that we are attempting to explain if we observe the proper quality of Catherine's doctrine. To the theologian who reads the *Dialogue*, these pages may often seem of ordinary value. All, or nearly all, that the saint teaches him, he already knows, and in a certain sense, he knows it better. His own reasoning has greater rigor, his essays more order, his style greater sobriety, not to mention that he scrutinizes the presuppositions and the doctrines of which Catherine has kept only the flower. But this theologian is not a good judge. Perhaps he has reached a point of familiarity with these doctrines that their immense meaning and astounding grandeur cease to impact him. He no longer perceives their force. Who knows if he has not come to find "normal" the affirmations which in reality are the most unexpected and the most divine? This is where Catherine surpasses the theologian. She knew, as if from within, the truth of the doctrines that she relates to us. Without having scrutinized them abstractly, she perceived their full meaning. These are two very different things. It is only too true that one may analyze basic knowledge most correctly and in a most scholarly manner, without touching, without testing, without perceiving the reality with which it is charged. Catherine, on the other hand, penetrates admirably right to the heart of this reality. Instead of her thoughts having been superimposed on her spirit, so to speak, they are as if born from a living, intellectual experience. The same conceptual ideas that others possessed she experienced with deep emotion. And it seems that during her whole life the progress of her knowledge consisted not in her changing ideas or acquiring new information about them, but really in the successive perception ever more penetrating and renewed: "O truth, ancient and new!..." We can then understand very well what her first biographers tell us regarding her infused knowledge. Granted that Catherine could well have received from elsewhere the material of her thought. But she has a way of appropriating it to herself beyond ordinary intelligence that depends on her entire soul and on God who inhabits it. Under divine influence, simple thoughts were transformed into conviction. From then on we wonder how far this directing power of knowledge will go. Henceforth intellect dictates action with a ten-fold force. Because truth was welcomed in all its fullness, it goes as far as expanding enthusiasm into action, where the initial concern for rectitude finds its conclusion and its reward.

⇑

We have been led to the same end by two distinct paths. The letters and the *Dialogue* attest to the essential role of knowledge in directing Catherine's life, i.e., the connection of doctrinal thought with her holiness and her apostolate. Many consequences emerge from the problem thus resolved. First of all, let us mention that a personality like St. Catherine's seems to be well understood only in the philosophical context of objective truth and intellect. For anyone who misjudges these values, reducing human life to a mere creation, without its having to conform to truth and intellect, the great Sienese saint is both an enigma and a challenge. Her experience renders ineffectual all attempts to explain the world in terms of pure emotion and idealism.

But a theologian may draw from the aforementioned conclusion yet another consequence. I would like to conclude by saying that theological knowledge has within itself a certain mystical value. Under the title of mystical theology we commonly designate today the relative knowledge of special and characteristic states of special souls:[5] their description, origin, effects, value, etc. We do not for a moment deny that there is here an object of distinct and passionate study. Psychologists have been able to apply themselves to this topic with their own methods, and we know what rich significance Bergson has recently recognized in the mystical experience. We cannot imagine that the theologian would not be able to judge this matter with similar success in so far as he alone possesses the full competence required of an object that involves the divine. But I want to note that this title and dignity of mystic belongs already to theology in a way that seems to me more profound. In truth, we are not sure that modern usage of the word theology does not contain a misunderstanding of what we are about to say. As far as we are concerned, theology is mystical by nature. It is of its nature to know the very truths that are actuated in the mystic. With this title of mystic, theology belongs to a movement and a vital creation. It is true that Catherine's case will seem exceptional. It is so, without any doubt, but only with regard to the actual method that she gave to her knowledge and not regarding its content. Up until now, few mystics have adopted the intellectual approach of theologians; but we think that all have done nothing less than to live their faith, whose science is theology. In this sense, the interpretation that we have given of Catherine, with reference to a theory of emotion and pure creation has perhaps a general significance. One would only avoid this in order to place the essence of the mystical life among extraordinary phenomena which also bear this name; but it is neither visions nor special revelations which constitutes the powerful allure of the mystics' lives. In the writings of Catherine, we may compare the space given to the account of her ecstasies with that given to a consideration of the common truths of faith. In reality, there is a similarity between these astonishing lives and the doctrines theologians teach in their books and in their schools. And what is most significant is that the mystic may not fail to recognize the aforementioned fact—once again, no!—in order to express for himself what he experiences, or even to have the right to experience it. Theology

---

[5] Such as the purgative, illuminative and unitive states. (Ed.)

has in itself the resources on which mysticism is founded. We are not unaware that knowledge proceeds in these great souls according to paths that are not those of the theologians, and we do not pretend that a St. Catherine herself has invested her entire intellect in these discussions. It remains that the mystics understood and penetrated precisely what the theologian teaches after he has grasped it to the best of his ability. The mystic and the theologian share a common objective. The greatness of the mystical life consists precisely in its being totally inspired by what the theologian teaches. And we would dare to say that the most natural movement of mystics, to which they yield in diverse ways, is to approach the theologian as the ordinary and dependable holder of the object which has always seduced them. In a word, we protest here against the isolation in which many people hold theology with relation to all that constitutes the beauty and power of life. Theology is made to serve them. It is fertile in works and holiness. Our honor is to be professors of the Christian life, and if the listener is so inclined, of the mystical life. Why do so many theologians not understand this better? In this, St. Catherine gives them a salutary and irrefutable lesson. Theology is knowledge of the most moving and powerful truths. It contemplates the God of love, creation, redemption, providence. It considers sin, grace, salvation. It sheds over the world and over life a new light—sweet light, as our saint says. It discloses for us things so beautiful and so solemn that no philosophy has conceived them, nor any poetry imagined them. Let us no longer be surprised that such a science is mystical by its nature, and that it incarnates itself, so to speak, from time to time in the course of the Christian eras, for our warning and our comfort, in living beings who are the honor of the human race, even as theology is the queen of the sciences.

2

Catherine of Siena: Doctor of the Church

Thomas McDermott, O.P.

It has been more than forty years since Pope Paul VI wrote *Mirabilis in Ecclesia Deus* in which he proclaimed the Virgin of Fontebranda a Doctor of the Church and expressed his hope that "the doctrine, method and learning of Catherine will bring it about that charity may soar in Christian hearts, and that…the desire for holiness may sharply increase among men and women everywhere."[1]

Despite continued interest in the life of St. Catherine, her "doctrine, method and learning" as found in the *Dialogue of Divine Providence*, her 381 extant letters and twenty-six prayers, is largely unknown outside of Italy. However, this situation may be changing and we could see the springtime of new engagement in Catherine's thought. Several recent publications give hope to such a renaissance. For example, we have recently witnessed the final translation into English of the entire Catherinian corpus;[2] the 2002 release of all her works, complete with a

---

[1] Pope Paul VI, Apostolic Letter The Title of Doctor of the Universal Church is Conferred on Saint Catherine of Siena *Mirabilis in Ecclesia Deus* (4 October 1970), §1, *Acta Apostolicae Sedis* 63:9 (30 September 1971), 674. An English translation can be found on my website www.drawnbylove.com .

[2] In 2008 the Arizona Centre for Medieval and Renaissance Studies published the fourth and final volume of Dominican Sister Suzanne Noffke's translation of Catherine's letters, bringing to completion her monumental translation project of the entire Catherinian corpus. Unless otherwise noted, the English translations of Catherine's works in this paper are taken from Noffke's translations: *Catherine of Siena. The Dialogue*, trans. and intro. Suzanne Noffke, OP (New York and Mahwah: Paulist Press, 1980); Catherine of Siena, *The Letters of Catherine of Siena*, trans. with notes Suzanne Noffke, OP, 4 vols. (Tempe, Arizona: Arizona Center for Medieval and Renaissance Studies, 2000-2008);

concordance on CD-ROM;[3] and the more recent arrival of my work entitled *Catherine of Siena: Spiritual development in her life and teaching-* -the first academic study in English that serves as a systematic guide to Catherine's mystical thought.[4]   Moreover, other recent developments such as the current interest in spirituality and mysticism, a new openness to doctrine and the patrimony of the Church, particularly among young English-speaking Catholics, and the renewed attention to the mystical experiences of Christian women—all contribute happily to this welcome revival.

As a modest contribution toward the fulfillment of Paul VI's hope and in an effort to present Catherine's rich and practical teaching, so long ignored, I propose to show how her life and teaching marvelously exemplify the goal of human existence as a dialogue or communion with the Father, Son and Holy Spirit *and* with our neighbor in the very heart of the Trinity. Her profound participation in the intimacy of Trinitarian life was actualized through her radical self-giving, self-forgetting love of neighbor in God. She has much to teach us about entering into divine and fraternal communion.   From this salutary lesson we will deduce the characteristics of her communion with others and her impact on them, her theological methodology, her special, unique way of "doing" theology, and her relevance for the world of today.

Communion with God

The goal of human existence as communion with the Trinity appears prominently in various places in the *Catechism of the Catholic Church*. For example, in no. 760 we read: "God created the world for the sake of communion with his divine life, a communion brought about by the 'convocation of men in Christ.'"[5]   Catherine makes this truth more

---

Catherine of Siena, *The Prayers of Catherine of Siena*. 2nd ed., ed., trans., notes Suzanne Noffke, OP (San Jose: Authors Choice Press, 2001).

[3] Cf. *Caterina da Siena, Santa Caterina da Siena: Opera omnia. Testi e concordanze. Recensione critica di testi: Letture a cura di Antonio Volpato; Dialogo e Orazioni a cura di Giulian Cavallini. Fausto Sbafoni, OP, coordinatore.* (Pistoia: Provincia Romana dei Frati Predicatori Centro Riviste, 2002). [CD-ROM]

[4] Written by myself and published by Paulist Press (New York) in 2008

[5] See *Catechism of the Catholic Church,* 2nd ed. (Washington DC: United States Catholic Conference, 2000), 1024, 1107, 1108, 1997.

explicit, showing us that the depth of our communion with the Father, Son and Holy Spirit is "mirrored" in the quality of our communion or relationship with others against the backdrop of the paschal mystery of Christ and his sheer surrender, absolute receptivity, infinite humble self-giving, and unreserved, unending *yes* to the Father.[6]

Catherine's communion with God first comes to light at the tender age of six when she experienced an attractive vision of Christ above the church of San Domenico in Siena. From then on her life can be regarded as an ever-increasing communion of mind and heart with Christ. She had a seemingly insatiable thirst to know him to such an extent, as she told her confessor, friend and biographer Raymond of Capua, that she believed herself to have been espoused to Christ.

The starting point of communion with God is found in Catherine's often repeated command to "lift the eye of the intellect" to the Crucified. In other words, we must cease all self-preoccupation and look upwards just as she did on that day long before, and see the God-Man whose blood is the indubitable sign of his infinite, self-giving love for us.

The cornerstone of her own life and teaching, Raymond says, was the fundamental maxim that the eternal Father revealed to her soon after she entered into seclusion in a small room or "cell" in her family house: "Do you know, daughter, who you are and who I am? If you know these two things you will have beatitude within your grasp. You are she who is not, and I AM HE WHO IS."[7] This is the beginning of Catherine's well-known doctrine on self-knowledge. Her spiritual thought is thereafter marked by a constant appeal to reason. Instead of demanding conformity of the will to a strict moral code, Catherine constantly enjoins us to "return to the cell of self-knowledge" which is the foundation of prayer for everyone from incipient to perfect.

Natural reason provides some understanding, but it is only by the light of faith that we can see the way to our divine destination of full

---

[6] Cf. Mary Ann Fatula, OP, *The Triune God of Christian Faith* (Collegeville, MN: The Liturgical Press, 1990), 60.

[7] Raymond of Capua, *The Life of Catherine of Siena*, trans. Conleth Kearns, OP (Wilmington, DE: Michael Glazier, 1980), §92. Kearn's work is a translation of Raimondo da Capua, *Legenda maior*. Bollandist *Acta Sanctorum.* (Paris: Palmé, 1866), Aprilis tomus 3: 826-967.

communion with the Three-in-One. This truth is encapsulated in her well-known image of "the eye of the intellect, the pupil of which is faith." It is knowledge, enlightened by faith, that allows us to see the truth—the all important truth—about ourselves and God: we are only creatures and apart from God we would cease to exist; the sin of our first parents has wounded us and our own sins have further darkened the eye of the intellect. These sobering truths are balanced by the truth about God: that out of love he made us in his own image and likeness, to be free and subject only to himself; through the infusion of his divine life he desires us to be "other christs;" the shedding of his blood makes known the endless immensity of his divine love for us.

The knowledge to which Catherine refers is the love-knowledge a lover has of the beloved. "Love follows knowledge" is a central theme in her spiritual thought.[8] Over and over again she reminds us that, "One who knows more, loves more".[9] The progression of knowledge and love which brings us into an ever-greater communion of intellect and will with the Trinity is the flowering of baptismal grace. By responding to the almost irresistible attraction of grace, our love of God and others deepens and expands. In the major section of the *Dialogue* called "The Bridge," this increase of knowledge and love transforms the pilgrim traveler from one who is initially possessed of merely slavish fear of God's punishment, then to the faithful servant whose love of God is mercenary and, at last, to the friend and the son or daughter of God who loves him in a completely disinterested way.

Although Catherine was a person of great passion who was described by one contemporary as "always joyful and of a happy spirit," she was distrustful of emotions as reliable indicators of progress on our spiritual journey.[10] "The reason [the soul] is joyful and glad," she says, "is that she has what she wanted. For it is characteristic of any love whatever to feel gladness [*allegrezza*] when one receives what one loves. So you cannot trust gladness in itself."[11]

---

[8] *Dialogue*, c. 1.

[9] *Dialogue*, c. 66.

[10] Testimony of Fra Tommaso Caffarini in M. H. Laurent, *Il processo Castellano con appendice di documenti.* Fontes vitae S. Catharinae senensis historici IX (Siena: Università di Siena, 1942), col. 1258.

[11] *Dialogue*, c. 106.

Sin is essentially a result of defective knowledge which leads to defective love of oneself, others and God. It acts like a cataract that covers over "the eye of the intellect, the pupil of which is faith" so that the intellect is darkened and truth cannot be seen as it really is. The root sin is selfish self-love, which is gradually chipped away as one learns the truth about oneself and God.

Communion with Others

The more our faculties of intellect and will are conformed to Christ's, the more he shares his divine life with us. As a result we are raised into an ever-greater communion with the Trinity, not as individuals but in communion with one another in Christ and in the Church. The Spirit of Christ draws us together in the Son and thus into the very being of God.

Catherine maintains a strong and persistent emphasis on charity toward others in her writings. Over and over again she stresses the importance of practical, self-effacing, self-donating love of neighbor. The eternal Father's repeated instruction on the bond between love of God and love of neighbor forms the basis of her conviction. "The soul, as soon as she comes to know Me, reaches out to love her neighbor."[12] Our first duty is to "reflect that God requires nothing else of us except we show our neighbors the love we have for God."[13] Having deeply assimilated this truth, Catherine writes to Ristoro di Piero Canigiani: "It is the nature of love...to love whatever the one we love loves."[14] In a letter to Raymond a few months before her death she says: "Love for our Creator cannot be sustained unless we love others for God's sake."[15] Catherine's emphatic teaching, conveyed through the image of a pregnant woman, is that our possession of the virtues can be verified only when they are put into action in our relationships with others.

> If a woman has conceived a child but never brings it to birth for people to see, her husband will consider himself childless. Just so, I [says the Eternal Father to Catherine] am the spouse of the soul, and unless she gives birth to the virtue she has conceived

---

[12] *Dialogue,* c. 89.

[13] Letter 89.

[14] Letter 299.

[15] Letter 343.

[by showing it] in her charity to her neighbors...then I insist that she has never in truth conceived virtue in her.[16]

It is God's design as well as a matter of justice that we love our neighbor, as the eternal Father tells her:

And because I loved you without being loved by you, even before you existed (in fact it was love that moved me to create you in my own image and likeness) you cannot repay me. But *you must give this love to other people*, loving them without being loved by them. You must love them without any concern for your own spiritual or material profit, but only for the glory and praise of my name, because I love them. In this way you will fulfill the whole commandment of the Law, which is to love me above all things and your neighbor as your very self.[17]

Catherine found an even stronger reason for reaching out to her neighbor when the eternal Father revealed to her that the quality of our love of neighbor reflects the quality of our love of God: souls "love their neighbors with the same love with which they love Me."[18] We see in Raymond's biography of Catherine, the *Legenda maior*, how her love of neighbor passed through stages commensurate with her progressive love of God: e.g., the "crisis" in the cell occasioned by the Lord's apparent withdrawal from her and her loss of consolations corresponds to the time the sick woman Andrea withdrew her affection from Catherine. In both cases Catherine perseveres in her love of God and neighbor. After she drinks the foul matter at Andrea's "open side," the Lord rewards her with the mystical slaking of her thirst at his open side. Our love of neighbor passes through the same stages as our love of God: slavish fear, mercenary love, and finally friendship and filial love.[19]

One event in Catherine's life contributed enormously to her conviction that divine and fraternal communion are inseparable, namely, when the Lord commanded her to leave the seclusion and consolations of her cell, where she had lived for three years, and join her family at the

---

[16] *Dialogue*, c. 11.

[17] *Dialogue*, c. 89. Emphasis mine.

[18] *Dialogue*, c. 60.

[19] Cf. "The Bridge," *Dialogue*, cc. 26-87.

dinner table. Years later she shared this experience with Raymond, telling him how she was traumatized and burst into tears, saying that the Lord was driving her away from him, that she did not want to be separated from him for even a moment, that meal times meant nothing to her, that she had turned her back on human companionship in order to find him, and that she had no desire to go back or do anything that might lead to her being separated from him. Here is part of the Lord's reply.

> *I have no intention whatever of parting you from myself, but rather of making sure to bind you to me all the closer, by the bond of your love for your neighbor.* Remember that I have laid down two commandments of love: love of me and love of neighbor. [...] It is the justice of these two commandments that I want you now to fulfill. On two feet you must walk my way; on two wings you must fly to heaven.[20]

As Cavallini says so pithily, the Lord impressed upon Catherine the reality that "the neighbor in fact is not a means of separation, but a means for a closer and more intimate contact with God."[21] Her decision to obey and leave her cell was momentous in her life.

Catherine's many mystical experiences, which go largely unrecorded in her own writings but which Raymond recounts in the *Legenda maior*, were far from being private and individualistic experiences. Each one represents a broadening and deepening of her outreach to neighbor as her communion with the Trinity intensifies. The *mystical espousals* (c. 1367), the highpoint of her seclusion in the cell, represent the union of Catherine's will with the divine will and the expectation that she would bring to birth many spiritual "children."[22] The *mystical exchange of hearts* (1370) was a further perfection of the union of wills which gave her a "boundless love of neighbor" for whom she was now prepared to die.[23] In the same year, the *mystical death* was a preparation for her entry into Christ's mission for the salvation of sinners through his

---

[20] Raymond of Capua, *The Life of Catherine of Siena*, §121. Emphasis mine.

[21] Giuliana Cavallini, "Caterina da Siena tra mistica e apostolato," *La patrona d'Italia: S. Caterina da Siena* XLIV:3 (maggio-giugno 1989): 9.

[22] Raymond of Capua, *The Life of Catherine of Siena*, §257.

[23] Raymond of Capua, *The Life of Catherine of Siena*, §182.

suffering and death.[24] The invisible *stigmata* (1375), which for Catherine corresponded to the "the marks of Jesus" received by St. Paul (Gal 6:7), signaled her definitive entrance into the passion and death of Christ for the salvation of sinners.[25] The *investiture vision* one year later represented the bestowal of a universal mission directed toward peace, conversion and Church reform.[26]

In Catherine's teaching the spiritual journey is never conceived as solitary or private but one that is made in communion with others, as seen in the eternal Father's words to her:

> You must gather together, as [my Son] said, either two or three or more. One alone is excluded from my companionship, since I cannot be "in the midst" of someone who has no companion. Those who are wrapped up in selfish love of themselves are alone, mere nothings, because they are cut off from my grace and from charity for their neighbors. And once deprived of me through their own fault, they turn to nothingness—for I alone am who I am. So those who are alone, those who are wrapped up in selfish love of themselves, are neither taken account of by my Truth nor acceptable to me.[27]

For her part, Catherine's cultured group of followers, called derisively by outsiders the *"Caterinati"* ("catherinized" ones) but whom she called her *"bella brigata"* or *"famiglia,"* many of whom were educated and drawn from the nobility, were constantly close to her heart as can be seen in her many prayers and supplications on their behalf right up to the moment of her death.

---

[24] Raymond of Capua, *The Life of Catherine of Siena*, §§212-213.

[25] Raymond of Capua, *The Life of Catherine of Siena*, §§194-195.

[26] Letter 219.

[27] *Dialogue*, c. 54. "Mankind does not realize his essence except by existing with someone, and even more profoundly and more completely, by existing for someone." John Paul II, General Audience of January 9, 1980. Internet: *http://www.vatican.va/holy_father/john_paul_ii/audiences/catechesis_genesis/d ocuments/hf_jp-ii_aud_19800109_en.html*

"Make yourself an instrument to give to everyone what they need"

In the *Dialogue,* the eternal Father commands Catherine to "make yourself an instrument [*mezzo*] to give to everyone what they need according to their disposition and as I, your Creator, will command you."[28] We have seen the importance of the neighbor in Catherine's spiritual thought; we will now look at the particular way in which she lived out her communion with the Trinity in her communion with others.

Before doing so, however, let us recall Catherine's tremendous impact on others. Numerous depositions made by her former followers in preparation for the canonization process, as well as statements by her biographer Raymond of Capua, describe Catherine as someone whom people simply enjoyed being around, how they felt better after listening to her, and how she could elicit the best from others. Fra Tommaso Caffarini, one of her devoted disciples and the major promoter of her cause, relates that "she had a special charm and as many people approached her, be they men or women, of every rank and of every profession, she made them all better and brought them back to God."[29] Described as the "mother of thousands of souls," Fra Bartolomeo Dominici, another disciple and former confessor of hers, testified to her effect on others:

> Who in fact could say enough about all the people and the types of people she brought back to a better life through her holy exhortations! How many noble matrons she induced to wear the religious habit! How many noble young women were moved by her words and the example of her life of virginity and the voluntary observance of extraordinary austerity! How many young men were converted and entered different Orders!

---

[28] "[F]a che tu sia uno mezzo di dare a ciascuno quello che lo' bisogna...." *Dialogue,* c. 109.

[29] Deposition of Fra Tommaso Caffarini in Giuseppe Tinagli, O.P., *Vita di Santa Caterina da Siena. Scritta da Fr. Tommaso Caffarini, discepolo della Santa,* a cura del P. Giuseppe Tinagli. Prefazione del P. Giacinto Laurent, O.P. (Siena: Ezio Cantagalli, 1938), 133. Critical edition: Thomas Antonii de Senis "Caffarini," *Libellus de Supplemento. Legende prolixe virginis beate Catherine de Senis.* Testi Cateriniani III, Centro Nazionale di Studi Cateriniani. Primum ediderunt Iuliana Cavallini, Imelda Foralosso (Roma: Edizioni Catheriniane, 1974), Book IV, c. 24.

How many religious she led to a better life! How many prostitutes she brought back to a chaste life! How many murderers and men who had gone astray through grave and old enmities did she reconcile with lasting peace, and owing to her holy admonitions were reunited in sincere and good friendship! It would take too long and in any case would seem incredible to tell how she, with her admirable speech, sweetly comforted the pious, frightened and confounded the arrogant and insolent; and not only the unlearned and the common people, but also princes, barons, solders, great prelates, illustrious doctors of the two laws, medical doctors and expert professors in Sacred Theology: in a few words she would ignite the more pious sentiments of the good people that spoke with her, miraculously and beneficially she confounded the crafty and bad ones.[30]

Within five years of leaving the seclusion of her cell, this lover of solitude and erstwhile recluse, who had vehemently protested when the Lord commanded her to re-enter the world, was so preoccupied with the salvation of souls that she now spoke of "eating and tasting" (*mangiatore e gustatore*) them. This unique Catherinian expression appears for the first time in one of her earliest extant letters: "You will learn to eat and savor souls, the food of God's servants, and there I advise and beg you to find your delight always."[31] So compulsory was her self-giving love of neighbor and no matter how deeply the person had descended into sin, saving souls was as important for her as eating food is for survival. Her desire to work for the salvation of souls, a desire which initially drew her to St. Dominic and the Order of Preachers, was augmented by a mystical experience she underwent shortly after leaving the cell when the Lord

---

[30] Innocenzo Taurisano, OP, *Santa Caterina da Siena nei ricordi dei discepoli: Fra Simone da Cortona, Don Stefano Maconi, Fra Bartolomeo Dominici* (Roma: Libreria Ferrari, 1957), 109-110. Italian translation of parts of the *Processo Castellano*.

[31] Letter 99 to Neri di Landoccio Pagliaresi, one of Catherine's earliest and closest disciples. Noffke dates the letter to February or March 1372. The expression "to eat and savor souls" appears more than twenty times in the letters and is an interpretation of Christ's words, "My food is to do the will of Him who sent me and to complete His work" (Jn 4:34). In his commentary on this passage (see Homily 34), Chrysostom says that just as we long to eat food, Christ longs for our salvation.

showed her the beauty of the soul of an old woman whom she was nursing. He said to her:

> "Look, dear daughter, at this soul. When it was already lost, I won it back through you. Is it not a thing of splendor? Would not anyone endure the greatest trials in order to win so exquisite a creature? I myself am Beauty Supreme from which all other beauty is derived. Yet so enchanting is the beauty of the souls of men that I gladly came down upon this earth and shed my Blood in order to redeem them. How much more should you yourselves take on you toil and labor for the sake of one another, so that so splendid a creature may not be lost? That is why I have given you a vision of this soul: to rouse you still more to spend yourself for the salvation of souls...."[32]

This vision of the soul's beauty prompted Catherine to ask God for a particular gift: the ability to see the state of the soul of anyone she would meet. The Lord granted the request.

Let us now examine the way in which Catherine lived out her fraternal communion as seen in the way in which she approached others in her letters and, indirectly, in her description of good bishops and superiors in the *Dialogue*. Among others of ordinary standing, we can identify six characteristics.

First, Catherine *loved others in God and for him* in that her love of neighbor was never apart or separate from her love of God. This is the fundamental principle of all her relationships with others. She explains it to Raymond in the *Legenda maior* using an analogy of plunging into a divine sea in which everything is seen through the medium of the water:

> Such a soul, she would say, neither sees nor loves either itself or any other created thing. It loses all remembrance of itself and of others. Upon my asking her to explain this she would say: "The soul which sees that it itself is nothing, and which knows that all its good is in its Creator, turns its back, with all the powers of its being, on itself and every creature, and plunges itself totally in its Creator. From [then] on it directs all

---

[32] Raymond of Capua, *The Life of Catherine of Siena*, §149.

it does, above all and throughout all, to him. Its whole mind is set on never going one step outside of him in whom it realises it has found its whole good and its complete and perfect happiness. This union of love grows daily more intense, and eventually the soul is, in a manner, so transformed into God that all its thoughts—its understanding and its love and its memory—are taken up exclusively with God, and busy about God alone. Itself and other creatures it sees only in God; it thinks of them and of itself exclusively in God. It is like what happens when a person dives into the sea and swims underwater. He sees nothing and touches nothing but the water and whatever is submerged in the water. Outside the water he sees nothing, feels nothing, and touches nothing. And if the images of the things outside fall in or on the water, he does not see them as they are in themselves, but only as they are or appear in the water. To envisage things in this way," continued Catherine, "means that love of self and of other creatures is now brought under the rule of right order, and can no longer stray beyond its proper bounds. It is now subjected to a rule which is divine. Existing and acting only in God, it no longer lusts after anything outside of God."[33]

Catherine also loved others "for God" in that everything she did was directed ultimately to giving God honor and glory. God *is* honored in the salvation of souls.[34] Her practical application of loving others in and for God appears in the *Dialogue* where the eternal Father instructs her:

If you have received my love sincerely without self-interest, you will drink your neighbor's love sincerely. It is just like a vessel that you fill at the fountain. If you take it out of the fountain to drink, the vessel is soon empty. But if you hold your vessel in the fountain while you drink, it will not get empty: Indeed, it will always be full. So the love of your neighbor,

---

[33] Raymond of Capua, *The Life of Catherine of Siena*, §100, pp. 92-93.

[34] "What these blessed ones want is to see me honored in you who are still on the way, pilgrims running ever nearer your end in death. Because they seek my honor they desire your salvation, and so they are constantly praying to me for you." *Dialogue*, c. 41. "The glory of God is man fully alive." Irenaeus, *Adv. haeres.* 4, 20, 7: PG 7/1, 1037.

whether spiritual or temporal, is meant to be drunk in me, without any self-interest.[35]

We know our love of neighbor is not perfect if we are jealous or distressed when we are not getting the return on our love that we want or when the one we love loves someone else more than ourselves.[36]

Catherine *identified with others,* even her enemies, and walked in solidarity with them. She advises us to "gently understand" others:

> And those vices that you seem to recognize in others, attribute them not only to them but to yourself, exercising true humility. And if indeed a person has a specific problem, he will correct it better after having been so gently understood, up to the point of his telling you the very thing you wanted to say to him.[37]

We are afforded an indirect insight into Catherine's own approach to others in her description of "good shepherds" (bishops and religious superiors) in the *Dialogue* where the theme of identification with others is prominent:

> In their love and hunger for souls they even laid down their lives to rescue them [the little sheep] from the devil's hands. They made themselves weak along with those who were weak. That is, to keep the weak from being confounded with despair and to give them more room to expose their weakness, they would show their own weakness, saying, "I am weak along with you." They wept with those who wept and rejoiced with those who rejoiced. Thus they knew how to give everyone the right food so tenderly. They encouraged the good by rejoicing in their goodness, for they were not gnawed up with envy but broad in the generosity of their own charity for their neighbors and subjects. [...] Those who were superiors became as subjects. They who were in authority became as servants. Though they were healthy, without the sickness and leprosy of deadly sin, they became as if afflicted. Though they were strong, they became as if weak. With the dull and simple they showed

---

[35] *Dialogue,* c. 64.

[36] Cf. *Dialogue,* c. 64.

[37] *Dialogue,* c. 102. My translation.

themselves as simple, and with the lowly, as lowly. And so with every sort of person they knew how to deal humbly and with charity, giving to everyone the right food.[38]

Examples abound in her letters where Catherine takes the side of the sinner, often by switching to the first person plural toward the end. Let it suffice to give just two examples. In her letter to Bérenger, an abbot and apostolic nuncio, she writes: "I your unworthy daughter have assumed and will continue to assume the debt of your sins myself. Your sins and mine we shall burn together in the fire of gentle charity, where they are consumed."[39] And to the parish priest at Asciano she writes:

We are ransomed servants; we can no longer sell ourselves. But when we are in deadly sin we do blindly sell ourselves to the devil. I beg you, for love of Christ crucified: let's get out of such slavery! I'll say no more, but let me tell you this much: my own sins are numberless. So I promise you that I will take both mine and yours and make of them a bundle of myrrh which I will keep in my breast with constant bitter weeping.[40]

Catherine strove to be *compassionate and not judgmental* as reflected in the eternal Father's words to her:

For often such a person's intention is good; there is no one who can judge the hidden heart. When you cannot see clearly and openly whether the sin is deadly, you must not pass judgment in your mind, but be concerned only about my will for that person. And if you do see it, you must respond not with judgment but with holy compassion.[41]

Give up judgment, which belongs to me, and take up compassion with hunger for my honor and the salvation of souls.[42]

---

[38] *Dialogue,* c. 119. Here Catherine expands on 1 Cor 9:19-23.

[39] Letter 109.

[40] Letter 24.

[41] *Dialogue,* c. 100.

[42] *Dialogue,* c. 103.

But I told you that it is not right for you to hand anyone over merely on the basis of what you see or feel within you or even what you see externally. Unless you have clearly seen the truth or have understood it through an explicit revelation from me, you are not to reprove anyone except in the manner I have already explained.[43]

Given the times in which she lived, Catherine is remarkably positive, hopeful and always mindful that the human person is made in the image and likeness of God.

In her writings and in the *Legenda maior*, there is ample evidence of how seriously Catherine objected to passing judgment on others. In his First Prologue to the work, Raymond says that "she ruled out of her life any passing of judgment on her neighbor, be it lawful or unlawful, and renounced all concern about how people might judge herself."[44] In the *Dialogue,* Catherine admits to the eternal Father of having once been judgmental of others, particularly priests:

You gave me as well a medicine against a hidden sickness I had not recognized, by teaching me that I can never sit in judgment on any person, especially on your servants. For I, blind and weak as I was from this sickness, have often judged others under the pretext of working for your honor and their salvation.[45]

She herself was the victim of intense criticism on the part of others, especially because of her singular way of life.[46]

---

[43] *Dialogue,* c.105.

[44] Raymond of Capua, *The Life of Catherine of Siena,* §12.

[45] *Dialogue,* c. 108.

[46] There is an autobiographical echo in the *Dialogue,* c. 100, when the eternal Father tells Catherine that souls who have clothed themselves in God's will "find joy in everything. They do not sit in judgment on my servants or anyone else, but rejoice in every situation and every way of living they see, saying, 'Thanks to you, eternal Father, that in your house there are so many dwelling places!' And they are happier to see many different ways than if they were to see everyone walking the same way, because this way they see the greatness of my goodness more fully revealed."

She insisted on *the necessity of fraternal correction* and was not slow in giving it, albeit in the best possible way and always with the objective of bringing about positive change.   Not to correct someone is nothing more than disguised selfish self-love.   She warns Gregory XI that the desire to merely "live in peace" with those in error "is often the greatest cruelty."[47] No one was exempt from her tough love; in fact, her friends, such as Raymond, were often the recipients of her sharpest rebukes. For example, she strongly chastised him when he decided, out of a legitimate fear of being killed, not to cross the border into France so as to deliver a message from Urban VI to Charles V, and called him "a child" who had been driven off and "willingly fled, very happy that God made concessions to your weakness!"[48]

In her dealings with others, Catherine *appeals to our human dignity*, made as we are in the divine image and likeness. In keeping with a certain tradition, she hardly mentions the Commandments but speaks often of the virtues and of the necessity of our "putting on virtue" after "having stripped" ourselves of vice, or "planting virtue" after having "dug out vice" with the "knife of conscience."[49] Sin is loathsome and repugnant, but human nature, although wounded by sin, still reflects the underlying beauty of the Creator.   "We love God and hate ourselves— not the self that is [God's] creation, but the self we see rebelling against our Creator."[50]

Catherine *adapts herself to individual persons and situations.*   Her principle here is stated in the *Dialogue* when the eternal Father tells her, "Reprove yourself if ever the devil or your own short-sightedness should do you the disservice of making you want to force all my servants to [go] the same way you yourself follow."[51] She strove to give "everyone the right food."[52] Her sensitivity to the uniqueness of each person and situation is seen most clearly in her letters, as noted by the Dominican Thomas Deman of *le Saulchoir* in his 1935 study:

---

[47] Letter 239.

[48] Letter 333.

[49] Cf. *Dialogue,* c. 23.

[50] Letter 101.

[51] *Dialogue,* c. 104.

[52] *Dialogue,* c. 119.

We must be careful that her resoluteness is not taken for rigidity: faithful to what she is thinking, she adapts the expression to the needs or capacities of her audience. She says the same thing, but she says it differently, according to whom she is writing (a Jew, a princess, a grieving mother, a religious): she possesses a gift of versatility and mobility, which is nothing else than a fine understanding of concrete situations and the consciousness of what is original in each particular case.[53]

Theological Method

Among all the Doctors, Catherine is unique in the fact that she was illiterate for most of her life and therefore her thoughts had to be dictated to others. Regardless of this fact, every Doctor of the Church is a theologian and has an "eminent doctrine," as Jean Galot, SJ, states:

The doctor is one who has set forth revealed doctrine manifesting deep *understanding* of this doctrine and giving it an *expression* worthy of admiration, so that a special charism of light granted by the Holy Spirit can be recognized in him. What distinguishes the charism of the doctor, in fact, is the excellence of the doctrine, the way in which he understands and expounds revelation. This charism implies an effort of doctrinal penetration, reflection and elucidation, with regard to the mysteries of the faith. This requires a certain *personal originality*, so that it is possible so to speak of a real contribution to doctrinal development.[54]

Catherine, like the other women Doctors, Sts. Teresa of Avila and Thérèse of Lisieux, presents religious truth not from the perspective of scholarship but rather from that of an intimately lived experience. I have described her elsewhere as a doctrinal mystical theologian who, like all genuine mystics, illuminates particular aspects of revelation afresh and

---

[53] Thomas Deman, O.P., "La théologie dans la vie de sainte Catherine de Sienne," *Supplément à la "Vie Spirituelle"* 1 Janvier 1935, [3]. See Chapter 1.

[54] Jean Galot, S.J., "Recognize the Charism in its Specific Value," *L'Osservatore Romano*: Weekly Edition in English, June 29, 1981, 2.

makes certain accepted but neglected truths astonishingly clear.[55] Her major work, the *Dialogue*, is an example of a type of private revelation known as a successive locution. Private revelation has a legitimate role in the Church, as stated in the *Catechism*: to assist the faithful in grasping more and more the full significance of Christ's definitive revelation and to help "live more fully by it in a certain period in history."[56]

What does this unlettered woman of the 14th century, whose writings Yves Congar, OP, nevertheless described as "incredibly dogmatic," have to say to theologians today?[57] First and foremost, an examination of her life and teaching shouts resoundingly to us that "doing" theology is essentially not a technique. Before talking about God, the theologian must be in communion with him. An approach to the truths of the faith that is rooted in contemplation is therefore necessary. Theologians who lack the authentic *gnosis* or love-knowledge of the Beloved which arises from contemplative union with God will produce defective or aberrant theologies, at best fixated on minutiae of no importance or at worst altogether false.

The fascinating story of the learned Franciscan theologian Lazzarino da Pisa, recounted by Fra Bartolomeo Dominici in his deposition, is a case in point. Jealous of Catherine's popularity among the Sienese, he sought her out only for the purpose of exposing heresy or ignorance on her part. But in the end Lazzarino is turned around by her and comes to realize that "he knew only the outer rind while she had penetrated the sweet essence."[58] Learned people, says the eternal Father in the *Dialogue*, often "neither see nor understand anything but the outer crust, the letter of Scripture. They receive it without any relish."[59] Catherine

---

[55] See McDermott, *Catherine of Siena. Spiritual development in her life and teaching* (New York: Paulist Press, 2008), 225.

[56] *Catechism of the Catholic Church*, 66-67.

[57] Yves Congar, OP, "Le Saint-Esprit dans les prières de Sainte Catherine de Sienne" in *Atti del Congresso Internazionale di Studi Cateriniani, Siena-Roma, 24-26 aprile 1980* (Roma: Curia Generalizia OP, 1981), 333. Online: http://www.centrostudicateriniani.it/download/Congresso_internazionale_di_s tudi%20cateriniani.pdf. See Chapter 4.

[58] Taurisano, *Santa Caterina da Siena nei ricordi dei discepoli*, 132-136; For an English translation, cf. McDermott, *Catherine of Siena*, 227-230.

[59] *Dialogue*, c. 124.

appreciates true learning but scorns learned people who "never understood learning because the horns of pride kept them from tasting its sweet marrow."[60] Ever the devoted disciple of "quell Paoluccio," she is entirely in sympathy with his criticism of those who are "ever learning and never attaining to knowledge of the truth" (2 Tim 3:7) and thus blow about like leaves in the wind.

Catherine reminds us of the importance of always keeping before us the full meaning of revealed truths, of "relishing" it, and never allowing ourselves to be lulled into complacency from over-familiarity with them. All truth is transformative, and God has revealed nothing of himself that is of no importance to us. Her penetration of the significance of doctrines such as the Incarnation, Redemption, and the human person's creation in *imago Dei* overflows in her zeal to make it known to others. Nowhere can her enthusiasm be seen more clearly than in her engrossment with the shedding of God's blood for us. The blood, for Catherine, was the key that unlocks for us the truth about God. It manifests the truth that is both ancient and *new*, as she says in a letter to a Carthusian:

> *His blood demonstrates the ancient truth revealed to us anew.* It is ancient in so far as we were in God's holy mind from eternity; it became new for us when God created us in his own image and likeness, giving us being so that we might enjoy his supreme eternal good, the good he has in himself. But *we didn't comprehend this new truth very well,* we didn't in truth believe that God had created us to give us eternal life. ... *[T]he blood revealed this truth to us anew.*[61]

Far from being a piece of inert information for Catherine, the blood of Christ, as the late English Dominican Kenelm Foster says, "expresses and symbolizes a positive active force; and to enter the blood is to enter the field of this force."[62] Catherine enjoins us to bathe, immerse, wash, nourish, satiate, fortify, drown, forget, warm, inebriate and clothe ourselves "in the blood."[63]

---

[60] *Dialogue,* c. 132.

[61] Letter 315. Emphasis mine.

[62] Kenelm Foster, O.P., "St. Catherine's Teaching on Christ," *Life of the Spirit* 16 (1962), 318-319. Online: www.drawnbylove.com.

[63] Cf. Letter 333 to Raymond of Capua.

This enthusiasm for the truths of the faith and refusal to become accustomed to them is noted by Deman:

> To the theologian who reads the *Dialogue*, these pages may often seem of ordinary value. All, or nearly all, that the saint teaches him, he already knows, and in a certain sense, he knows it better. His own reasoning has greater rigor, his essays more order, his style greater sobriety, not to mention that he scrutinizes the presuppositions and the doctrines of which Catherine has kept only the flower. But this theologian is not a good judge. Perhaps he has reached a point of familiarity with these doctrines that their immense meaning and astounding grandeur cease to impact him. He no longer perceives their force. Who knows if he has not come to find "normal" the affirmations which in reality are the most unexpected and the most divine? This is where Catherine surpasses the theologian. She knew, as if from within, the truth of the doctrines that she relates to us. Without having scrutinized them abstractly, she perceived their full meaning. These are two very different things. It is only too true that one may analyze basic knowledge most correctly and in a most scholarly manner, without touching, without experiencing, without perceiving the reality with which it is charged. Catherine, on the other hand, penetrates admirably right to the heart of this reality.[64]

Having perceived the "full meaning" of religious truth and relished it, Catherine was impelled to communicate it to others in an array of continually changing images of walled cities, pasta, hearths, burning logs, worms, nursing infants, casks of wine, roasting lambs, tables, eagles, pregnant women, etc.

The theologian can learn yet another lesson from Catherine. Anyone who studies her works soon realizes that there is always an ecclesial orientation. She never comes across as isolated from the Body of Christ or as someone seeking originality at any cost. Instead, she is the daughter of a tradition which she echoes joyfully in her own sunny Italian way. This is not surprising because, as the contemporary spiritual writer Jacques Philippe says, "contemplation brings us into the heart of the mystery of the Church.... The grace of prayer always

---

[64] Pp. 15-16.

integrates the one praying more fully into the mystery of the Church."[65] Catherine's increased concern for the moral and spiritual reform of the Church reflects a deepened interiority and realization of her spousal relationship with Christ and, therefore, with his Body the Church. The further we pass along the Christ-Bridge, she says, the more we are concerned with the honor of God, the salvation of souls and the reform of the Church.[66]

Her solidarity with others, communion with the Church, tireless self-giving, renunciation of all egoism, and spirit of wholehearted forgiveness can all be glimpsed in a remarkable passage in a letter to Raymond. Believing that Pope Gregory XI was angry with her, Catherine, not wanting to annoy him further, asked Raymond to communicate to him the following message:

> Holiest Father, punish me, but punish me in reason, not in anger. With whom shall I take refuge if you forsake me? Who else will support me? To whom shall I go if you banish me? My persecutors hunt me and I flee to you and to the other children and servants of God. And were you to leave me and no more to care for me, but to be angry with me, I would hide myself in the wounds of Christ (you are His Vicar); and I know that He will receive me, for He wills not the death of a sinner. And when I had been received by Him you would not send me away, but we would stand together, each in his own place and fight courageously with the weapons of virtue for the sweet Bride of Christ.[67]

Relevance Today

Pope John Paul II made the following observation in his apostolic letter *Novo millennio ineunte* at the close of the jubilee year 2000:

> Is it not one of the "signs of the times" that in today's world, despite widespread secularization, there is *a widespread*

---

[65] Jacques Philippe, *Time for God* (New York: Scepter, 2008), 77.

[66] Cf. *Dialogue*, c. 133.

[67] Letter 267 quoted in Johannes Jorgensen, *Saint Catherine of Siena* (London, New York, Toronto: Longmans, Green and Co., 1938), 278-279.

demand for spirituality, a demand which expresses itself in large part as *a renewed need for prayer?* Other religions, which are now widely present in ancient Christian lands, offer their own responses to this need, and sometimes they do so in appealing ways. But we who have received the grace of believing in Christ, the revealer of the Father and the Savior of the world, have a duty to show to what depths the relationship with Christ can lead. The great mystical tradition of the Church of both East and West has much to say in this regard. It shows how prayer can progress, as a genuine dialogue of love, to the point of rendering the person wholly possessed by the divine Beloved, vibrating at the Spirit's touch, resting filially within the Father's heart.[68]

Catherine, a layperson whose writings were intended not for cloistered religious but for everyone, stands out in the history of the Church as someone "wholly possessed by the divine Beloved" who shows us, perhaps even more by her life than by her marvelous doctrine, "to what depths the relationship of Christ can lead." Although she lived long ago, she validates for our time, as she did for her own, the path that Jesus himself trod and is a supreme example of the thomistic axiom that grace elevates nature and takes away nothing of value.[69]

Before the Second Vatican Council, Karl Rahner, SJ, expressed the hope that in the future spirituality would be more theological and theology more spiritual. Catherine has a contribution to make in the realization of this hope. She answers and informs the demand today for a "lived theology,"[70] a theology that is not disconnected from life. We have already spoken of the way in which she points theologians toward a

---

[68] John Paul II, Apostolic Letter at the Close of the Great Jubilee of the Year 2000 *Novo millennio ineunte* (6 January, 2001), §33. Online: *http://www.vatican.va/holy_father/john_paul_ii/apost_letters/documents/hf_jp-ii_apl_20010106_novo-millennio-ineunte_en.html*

[69] Cf. John Paul II, Apostolic Letter On the Occasion of the Six-Hundredth Anniversary of the Death of St. Catherine of Siena *Amantissima Providentia*. English translation from *L'Osservatore Romano*, Weekly Edition in English, June 23, 1980, 7. Online: www.drawnbylove.com.

[70] The expression "lived theology" is from John Paul II, *Nuovo millennio ineunte*, 27.

more contemplative approach to theology but she also serves as a corrective to the various strands of contemporary spiritualities whether they are rooted in Christianity or not. Often intellectually shallow and individualistic, the emphasis is frequently on lived experience separated from reason, resulting in a kind of spiritual narcissism in which one is preoccupied with a quest for "personal fulfillment," "authentic existence," "becoming fully alive," and "higher states of consciousness" that is contrary to Catherine's absolute surrender, total gift of self, and complete receptivity to the three divine Persons of the Trinity mirrored in her communion with others and expounded in her teachings.

Evelyn Underhill, in her renowned work *Mysticism: A study in the nature and development of spiritual consciousness*, attests to the fact that Catherine's life and teaching merit attention:

> The true successor of Dante as a revealer of Reality, and next to St. Francis the greatest of Italian mystics, Catherine exhibits the unitive life in its richest, most perfect form. She was a great active and a great ecstatic: at once politician, teacher, and contemplative, holding a steady balance between the inner and the outer life. Well named, "the mother of thousands of souls," with little education she yet contrived, in a short career dogged by persistent ill-health, to change the course of history, rejuvenate religion, and compose, in her "Divine Dialogue," one of the jewels of Italian religious literature.[71]

Let us hope that in the years ahead Catherine's rich spiritual teaching will receive the attention which it has always deserved and which is so long overdue.

---

[71] Evelyn Underhill, *Mysticism. A study in the nature and development of man's spiritual consciousness* (New York: Dutton, 1930), 467.

3

Freedom and Politics in St. Catherine of Siena

Maria Francesca Carnea

During the Middle Ages the world found it needed a spirituality which would compensate trials with hope, ease mourning with comfort, redeem the "prose" of labor with the "poetry" of faith and find an answer to life's brevity in an unending afterlife.[1]

Florence, in central Tuscany, had from early times organized itself into a commune. It was a natural place for commerce and culture to emerge, also politics—through the internal strife of Guelphs and Ghibellines. It rose to pre-eminence in the region and beyond, and its golden period was during the 13th to 15th centuries. Dante, Giotto, Donatello, Leonardo and Savonarola were among its luminaries. The mid-14th century Catherine of Siena[2] ranks with them. Fired by great

---

[1] Cf. W. Durant, da: *Storia della Civiltà. Il mondo medievale*, vol. I, *L'epoca della fede*, tomo III, ed. Araba Fenice, Cuneo, 1995, p. 384. [English translation of this work: *The Story of Civilization,* 11 vols. New York: Simon and Schuster, 1935-75. All notes in brackets with "-Ed." are mine.]

[2] In relation to this historical period, please refer to the following works: A. Capecelatro, *Storia di Santa Caterina da Siena e del Papato nel suo tempo* (5th ed.), Tip. Liturgica di S. Giovanni Deseleé, Le Febbre e Cia, Roma, 1886; E. Dupré-Theseider, *I Papi di Avignone e la questione romana, F. le Monnier,* Firenze, 1939; E. Dupré-Theseider, *Il Medioevo come periodo storico*, Patron, Bologna, 1968; E. Dupré-Theseider, "*Roma dal Comune di popolo alla Signoria pontificia (1252-1377),*" in *Storia di Roma*, vol. XI, Istituto di Studi Romani, ed. Cappelli, Bologna, 1952; L. Gatto, "*La Roma di Caterina,*" in *La Roma di Santa Caterina da Siena*, ed. M. G. Bianco, Quad. L.U.M.S.A., Ed. Studium, Roma, 2001; L. Gatto, *Viaggio intorno al concetto di Medioevo*, Bulzoni, Roma, 1995; L. Gatto, *Storia di Roma nel Medioevo*, Roma, 1999; I. Taurisano, *L'ambiente storico cateriniano. Siena, Firenze, Roma.* Amatrice (Rieti), Scuola Tip. Dell'orf. Masch.,

religious conviction and a deep love for her own country, she saw that the world around her was "without peace and without light." She sensed around her the rumblings of rebellion, the horrors of war and the cry of wickedness.[3] At the beginning of the 14th century there was a bitter struggle to wrest spiritual rule away from Rome. Philip the Fair, in his boundless pride and hatred of Pope Boniface VIII, was overjoyed when on June5, 1305, after the brief pontificate of Benedict XI, Bertrand de Goth, Archbishop of Bordeaux, was elected as Pope Clement V. There had been French popes before. Christendom had no suspicions of what was to happen when, instead of setting out for Rome, Clement V took the road to Avignon. In the three following elections, twenty-three out of twenty-four electing cardinals were French. Christianity suddenly became aware that it stood in great danger of the papacy finding a new seat on the other side of the Alps, and began persistently to ask for a return to Rome.

The fame of Catherine's extraordinary virtue and her vigorous calls to the pope to return to his city, her prolonged fasts, her daily communions, her ecstasies, her letters[4] written to persons of great influence, her admonishments of evil-doers who oppressed the people and kept the pope far from Rome, "scandalized" Christendom and could not be tolerated. This woman's voice, which could well draw proselytes, had to be silenced. What business was it of hers, the reform or government of the Church? It was her business to pray (and to do so in silence), and to nurse the sick: politics, reforms, peace and war were affairs for men, not women. So she was sent to Florence to mend her ways. Here, however, her popularity was so great that in 1376 she was called to be

---

1934; I. Taurisano, *S. Caterina da Siena, Patrona primaria d'Italia. La sua eroica pazienza, le sue preghiere per la Chiesa e per il Pontefice*, Libreria Ferrari, Roma, 1956; I. Taurisano, *S. Caterina e il ritorno del Papa a Roma*. Ottavario di Meditazioni in onore di S. Caterina da Siena, Vergine dell'Ordine di S. Domenico, presso la direzione del Rosario Memorie Domenicane, Roma 1898.

[3] Cf. I. Taurisano, *L'ambiente* ..., cit., pp. 57-67.

[4] Cf. L. Ferretti, *Letter e di S. Caterina da Siena, Vergine Domenicana*, tip. S. Caterina da Siena, 1918, vol. 5. Citations to the Letter s henceforth abbreviated Letter [All of Catherine's letters have been translated in English. Cf. *The Letters of Catherine of Siena*, translated with introduction and notes by Suzanne Noffke, O.P. (Tempe, AZ: Arizona Center for Medieval and Renaissance Studies, 2000-2008).]

ambassador to Avignon, where she was partly responsible for the papacy's return to Rome.

We get to know Catherine through her letters, sent to Popes Gregory XI and Urban VI, Charles V of France, Queen Joan of Naples, the Duke of Anjou, the king of Hungary and many cardinals, bishops, statesmen, brothers, sisters, family friends and artists, and ordinary men and women. No one could resist her ardor, the witness of her charity, or even her reproofs when they were needed,[5] such as this one she wrote to Joan of Naples, "No riches or grand estate, no worldly dignity, no baron or people who are your bodily subjects will be able to defend you against the supreme Judge, or save you from divine justice."[6]

Her teaching was adapted to the different social levels of people whom she knew and accepted just as they were in themselves, whether she was dealing with the mother of a family, or a priest, a gentleman or a poor artisan; asking only that each should be faithful to the duties of their state of life.[7] States of soul were even more different than their exterior circumstances, and Catherine took account of this. She writes that, "the city of the soul has three main gates; memory, intellect and will. Our creator allows these gates to be attacked, and sometimes to be taken by storm, with one exception, that of the will. The intellect often sees only darkness, the memory is full of frivolous and passing things, of confused and dishonest thoughts, the senses are the prey of uncontrolled feelings. The door of the will is so strong that no creature or demon can open it if the doorkeeper does not consent. So keep it firmly shut, and your soul will be a city that is always free."[8]

Having, as few others did, a lively awareness of her freedom and autonomy, Catherine felt at every moment part of the entire body of Christianity and responsible for the evils afflicting the Church; and so she labored intensively for its reform.[9] What did Catherine mean by the reform and renewal of the Church? Certainly not the overthrow of its

---

[5] Cf. I. Taurisano, *S. Caterina e il ritorno* ..., cit., pp. 30-31.

[6] Letter 317, vol. IV, pp. 434-445, to the queen of Naples.

[7] Cf. I. Taurisano, *S. Caterina e il ritorno* ..., cit., pp. 31; 66; 105-106.

[8] Letter 313, vol. IV, pp. 399-409, to the count of Fordi.

[9] *Cf.* Adriana Cartotti Oddasso, "La Santa di Fontebranda e l'obbedienza," *Oss. Romano*, 30 aprile 1971.

essential structures, rebellion against its pastors, and an open path to personal charisms, arbitrary innovations in liturgy and discipline. On the contrary, she repeatedly stated that the full beauty of the bride of Christ would return, if reform was made "not by war but by peace and quiet, by humble and continuous prayer, by the blood and sweat of God's servants."[10] We are talking about a reform that is primarily interior and then exterior, but "always in communion with and in filial obedience to Christ's lawful representatives."[11]

A Look at Society in the Middle Ages

To appreciate Catherine's life not only interiorly but also from the point of view of her relevance to the papacy and to society, we need to look at the times in which she lived.[12] A quick glance at the middle of the 14th century clearly shows us the one fact dominating other events; the papacy, which from St. Peter onwards had been established in Rome for fourteen centuries, had been transferred to Avignon in France. Italians began to call this the papacy's "Babylonian Captivity",[13] and luminaries like Dante and Petrarch began to agitate for the return of the papacy to Rome, "which used to have two suns, the pope and the emperor."

Philip the Fair completely dominated Clement V, and it could be said that Clement's pontificate was the Church's real "captivity;" John XXII was more energetic in the pursuit of his own policies. After the death of Philip the Fair, France had less influence, and Benedict XII had serious thoughts of returning to Italy. But the College of Cardinals was dominated by the French, and an outbreak of hostilities between France and England laid a moral commitment on the pope and his successors to remain in Avignon in order to negotiate an end to this war which was impeding the Crusades, so important to the Church. A return to Italy and

---

[10] Cf. Angiolo Puccetti, *S. Caterina da Siena. Il Dialogo della Divina Provvidenza*, ed. Cantagalli, Siena, 1992, chap.15, pp. 57-59; chap. 86, pp. 173-175. Henceforth abbreviated as *Dialogue*.

[11] Cf. A. Samorè, *S. Caterina, la Chiesa e il Papa*, Quaderni Cateriniani, n. 4, ed. Cantagalli, Siena, 1971, p. 10.

[12] Cf. A. Capecelatro, *Storia di S. Caterina ...*, cit., p. 8.

[13] Cf. E. Duprè-Theseider, *Roma dal Comune ...*, cit., p. 714.

the difficulties foreseen in re-establishing a secure papal authority over its restless population was not an inviting prospect.[14]

Avignon was purchased from Joan of Naples[15] on June 12, 1348 for 80,000 florins, and became the established legal seat of the Church. It was enriched with sumptuous houses and sacred buildings; the papal palace was magnificently enhanced and refurbished.[16] The pontificates of Clement VI and Innocent VI were passed here. With the disastrous end of the first period of the Hundred Years' War, the political influence of the House of Anjou was partly diminished, and France's growing moral and political power was brought to a standstill. There was a growing conviction that a return to Rome was possible, and a tentative attempt was made by Urban V, but the definitive return was made by Gregory XI in 1377.[17]

When we look at the attitude of the Avignon popes to the question of returning to Rome, we have to recognize that none of them (with the exception of Clement VI perhaps) ruled out the possibility. There was no easy solution; indeed, it called for a change of position in the whole western political situation. It touched upon essential and important points in the whole life of the Church, such as its sovereignty in Italy and its temporal independence throughout the countries of Christendom, the relationship between the papacy and the college of cardinals, and between the Curia and the people of Italy, who, in their great exasperation, were threatening a schism. International political issues had to be addressed, like the settlement of the French-English conflict, the struggle against mercenary armies and preparation for the crusades. A whole series of interdependent problems had been created, which could only find a solution by the abandonment of Avignon.[18]

All this may be summed up in a single phrase, "the Roman question;" making use of a formula which, five centuries later, would signify the problem of relationship between state and Church. To use it of the 14th

---

[14] Cf. E. Duprè-Theseider, *I Papi* ..., cit., pp. X-XI (introduction).

[15] It was certainly an important transaction for the Curia, but at that moment the beautiful queen, a notorious sinner, needed all of the Pope's indulgence.

[16] Cf. E. Duprè-Theseider, *Roma dal Comune* ..., cit., p. 630.

[17] Cf. E. Duprè-Theseider, *I Papi...*, cit., p. XI (introduction).

[18] Cf. E. Duprè-Theseider, *I Papi...*, cit., p. XXXVIII (introduction).

century is not inappropriate, because from then on the first national kingdoms, partly autonomous because they recognized no superior, were confronting the problem of their relationship with the Church.

To regain its full ascendancy over the Christian world, the papacy had to return to Rome and sever its relationship with the kingdom of France. There were indeed many difficulties, but also a prophetic atmosphere, revelations, an eschatological vision which tended to favor a return to Rome, and saw it as part of a process pre-established by Providence.

After Pope Urban V's failed attempt to return to Rome, and the countless counter-arguments for making the move, it seemed a miracle of Providence when, on January 17, 1377, Gregory XI actually arrived in Rome to take up his definitive residence. This pope had been induced to make the final decision, at least partly, by the words of St Catherine of Siena;[19] indeed, his good intentions to return to Rome were not resulting in action, and Catherine could see papal power rapidly crumbling away, and the Italian population's spiritual detachment from the Church. The pope had to return to Rome as soon as possible. She therefore sent a letter to Gregory XI;[20] its courageous severity is amazing. The exhortation to "kill the rat of self-love; it is a rat that gnaws and severs the roots of our tree" has a precise meaning, because he was notoriously indulgent towards his own relations and their representatives in Italy.

Catherine teaches us that we need to know how to be firm in our resolutions; and she would utter the maxim, "Sometimes affection for one's family is the greatest cruelty." Every single letter she sent to the pope urged him to "behave manfully" (whereas all those she would later send to the more choleric Urban VI invited him to be calm and indulgent). To hasten his return, she made the important decision to meet the entire curia and overcome the pope's last resistances, he himself not having the fortitude to confront the obstacles they were putting in his way.[21] A single confrontation convinced him that his return to Rome was God's will.[22]

---

[19] Cf. E. Duprè-Theseider, *I Papi...*, cit., p. XXXIX-XL (introduction).

[20] Letter 185, vol. III, pp. 158-167, to Gregory XI.

[21] Cf. E. Duprè-Theseider, *I Papi ...*, cit., pp. 204-207.

[22] Cf. A. Alessandrini, *Il ritorno dei Papi da Avignone e S.Caterina da Siena*, Arch. Deput. romana stor. p. LVI (1933).

In Catherinian tradition there is one more episode: the departure for Rome had already been decided, ships from Genoa, Venice and Naples were waiting; and around the pope the last battle was waging. The cardinals, the people of Avignon and the pope's relations were imploring him, threatening him and beseeching him to remain. Gregory XI summoned Catherine, not for advice, but to command her under obedience to reveal God's will to him. Catherine then took counsel with her own conscience, and reminded him of his secret vow, made as a cardinal and of which he had never spoken, to return the papacy to Rome if he were elected pope. Gregory bowed to this decisive revelation of the divine will.[23] On January 17, 1377, after a last stop at Corneto,[24] Gregory XI set foot in Rome with the intention of remaining, and there he died on March, 27, 1378. An Italian, Urban VI, was elected pope. The cardinals who had never accepted the idea of leaving Avignon forever took revenge by proceeding to the election of a second pope, Robert of Geneva, who took the name of Clement VII.[25]

The schism caused by the Avignon cardinals rebelling against the Italian pope divided the whole of Europe into two camps and two "obediences," one devoted to the pope of Rome, the other to the antipope at Avignon.[26] Only with Martin V, of the House of Colonna, would the helm of St Peter's boat be taken firmly in hand and the Church definitively become a territorial entity among the Italian States.

---

[23] This episode is recounted in the deposition of Fra Tommaso Caffarini in the "Processo" for the canonization of St. Catherine of Siena. Cf. I. Taurisano, "S. Caterina e il ritorno del papato a Roma," *Memorie domenicane*, 1929.

[24] Catherine writes a letter to the Pope while he is in Corneto: Letter 252, vol. IV, pp. 49-54

[25] Salutati, Ep. X, 4, identifies exactly the political motives of this schismatic second election, "*vel odi uominis italici, vel studio proprie nationis, vel summi pontificatus ambitione*" ["either because of the hatred of the Italian man, or by zeal for one's nation, or by the ambition of the supreme Pontiff."] More simply, *Cron. Di Pisa* (R.I.S., XV, col. 1075) says: "*perocché lo papa li aveva ammoniti e corretti di cose che non erano dovute, elli sì li appuoseno che non era vero papa, e voleano andasse a tener la corte a Vignone, perché la maggior parte delli cardinali erano franciosi*" ["because the pope had admonished them and corrected the things that were needed, they claimed he was not the true pope and wished to take the court to Avignon because most of the cardinals were French."]

[26] Cf. E. Duprè Theseider, *I Papi* ..., cit., p. 234.

Her Teaching about Freedom and Politics

We could ask ourselves at this point what kind of intervention a simple woman like Catherine could make, and what tasks could have been entrusted to her. We find an answer indicated in the passage in Matthew's gospel where he says that God keeps his secret designs hidden from the wise and prudent, and reveals them to mere children (Mt 11:25);[27] the person who has faith is great.

It is certain that Catherine, without having had any human teacher, was so richly endowed by God with "the gifts of wisdom and knowledge" (1 Cor 12:2), that she became a most effective teacher of life. She was not only a great contemplative who had the highest mystical experiences, but was, at the same time, a woman of action, ready to commit all the gifts of her intelligence, heart and will to many social activities. She was simultaneously a woman of prayer and of action; action that was unusual for a woman of the people during the Middle Ages. Her works went beyond assistance and other works of charity; she intervened as a peacemaker between peoples, and in diplomatic negotiations between rulers and the Holy See.

Her political thought had, as its foundation and starting point, recognition of the value and dignity of the human person, and of society's role in the eternal destiny of the human person. According to Catherine, the function of civil society was to be at the service of its members, and therefore had no other end than that of encouraging and making possible their full personal development. For her, the aim of society was not the interests of groups, factions or parties, but "the universal common good" which guaranteed an orderly development of social life. The first and indispensable task for rulers was to be able to govern themselves. The important virtues they needed for this end were charity and justice.[28]

---

[27] Cf. B. Mondin, "Cultura cristiana e missione storica dell'Europa," in *Filosofia e Cultura nell'Europa di Domani*, B. Mondin (ed.), Città Nuova Editrice, Roma, 1993, p. 38. Cf. G. Cottier, "I valori che hanno fatto l'Europa," in *Il nuovo areopago*, n. 35, 1990, p. 26.

[28] Cf. M. Liana Mattei, "Pensiero Politico di Caterina - un'eredità per oggi," in *Ave Maria. Bollettino Bim. della Congr. delle Suore Domenicane di S. Caterina da Siena*, October 1995, pp. 111-113.

Catherine therefore occupies one of the first places among the protagonists of history. She was fully intent on following a work that was not in itself of primarily religious character, but concerned political rights, reconciliation and peace.[29] She overthrew all the social conventions of her time, as well as the mental (and ecclesiastical) restrictions on women, and placed herself on all fronts where men were fighting for truth, justice and peace, judging nothing to be impossible, or too difficult or unsuitable to her position as a woman of the people, and, moreover, illiterate.[30]

Catherine undertook a vast work of peacemaking.[31] John-Paul II said of her that she truly "knew the word of reconciliation" and spoke it at a time that was difficult for the Church and for the world. Her work of conciliation and of peace not only encompasses Siena and Italy, but, one might say, the whole of Europe. She certainly had a wide vision of her mission and, it could be said, of the European mentality, which she had absorbed from childhood in her native city.

We who live in the 21st century, subjected to a mentality of aggressive nationalism and whose political frontiers have become barriers, do not find it easy to visualize a Europe in which all considered themselves in some way citizens of what was, or had been, an empire, and who moved around freely from one country to another. Siena itself was one of the many city-states of that era, and was in commercial relationship with most of central Europe. Latin was still the official common language across most of the West, in spite of the increasing popularization of vernacular languages. European culture was unified, notwithstanding political and social divisions. While all cherished their

---

[29] Cf. M. Castellano, "S. Caterina da Siena e l'Europa" in *Quaderni. Cateriniani* n° 30, ed. Cantagalli, Siena, 1985, p. 3.

[30] Cf. G. Anodal (ed.), *S. Caterina da Siena. Patrona d'Italia, una sfida per la donna di oggi*; ed. Studio Domenicano, 1990, pp. 86-87.

[31] If her early youth was a time of tender, intimate colloquies with Christ in the cell within her home, by the time she had matured it was that of great temptations in which Catherine had learned that virtue is acquired and perfected in the crucible of trials as Jesus invited her to return to live in the midst people, to descend directly and personally to that "battlefield" that is the world. Jesus reminds us through Catherine that by "two feet" and "two wings" (love of God and neighbor) one goes to God. Cf. G. Anodal (ed.), *S. Caterina...*, cit., p. 157.

own nationality (which was becoming more accentuated), people of the 14th century did not yet consider each other as foreigners, but as co-involved in a common destiny; and had no difficulty in living together.

Catherine had before her a Europe that was politically divided, but which was united in a human and Christian culture shaped by the preceding centuries;[32] and, in a century that was very difficult and full of events which lacerated even the ecclesial structure from within, she knew how to point out the way to conciliation and order.

Her teaching was what we might call a political philosophy, and today more than ever we are aware of the need to rediscover the purity of ethics, politics and philosophy. Her teaching and exhortations were about purity of intent in political life, of moral strength, wide horizons and a strong sense of the common good.[33] "It seems that God inspires her to great dignity and dialectical force to the point of controversy, being very competitive, exasperatingly reminding the rulers of the earth of their binding agreements so as to obtain valid results for the good of the Church, of society and of good governance for the community."[34] We could say that, under God's inspiration, she was an extremely dignified and powerful speaker, very competitive, at times an exasperatingly hard bargainer with the great ones of the earth in order to obtain practical results for the Church's cause, for society, for the world, for the good government of the masses.

In letter after letter she extols memory, intelligence and the heart, human feelings. All these factors, which are components of human spiritual personality, combine to shape the will. Catherine is totally convinced about human free will; this results in her being very rigorous in the moral sphere, because, as she cannot accept that we are anything

---

[32] Cf. M. Castellano, *S. Caterina* ..., cit., pp. 4-7.

[33] Letter 367, to the Signori of Siena in which she desired to see that "the pearl of holy justice [would] shine always within your breasts, to rise above all self-love and attend to the universal good of your city and not paying attention to your own particular good" ["*La margarita della giustizia sempre riluca nei petti vostri, lavandovi da ogni amor proprio, attenendo al bene universale della vostra città e non propriamente al bene particolare di voi medesimi*"], vol. V, pp. 279-284

[34] Cf. P. Pajardi, *Caterina la Santa della Politica*, ed. Martello, Milano, 1993, pp. 9; 11; 13; 62.

but absolutely free, as willed by God the Creator, the consequence is that we have to accept the guilt for every deviation from the moral code. Because of this, though she was overwhelmingly indulgent when faced with penitence and conversion, her moral judgments were rigorous in the extreme. Just as she idealized everything, she idealized action as an active projection of the will; the will produces action, and action produces results.

Each person receives specific talents, and no others, and consequently there is no one measure of perfection for all. Each one has a maximum potential in a specific human situation (and on this she is particularly insistent). This is a realistic concept of human responsibility for personal perfection.

At times, Catherine may seem absolutist and fundamentalist, even arrogant, yet in reality she was profoundly humble and had a great sense of the human situation as it really is. She can give the impression of being "utopian," and indeed, expresses an infinite ambition for each person to give the best of themselves, spurred onward by the will.[35] She insists on "commitment." Each one must act according to individual strengths; human beings have to take advantage of their individual talents. She turns the idea of the will around: the will is not mere intention, but intention followed by committed behavior,[36] not just external behavior, either, although this is important, but above all a deep interior attitude of mind and heart.

She wants to show how what gives us choice, which is the use of freedom, or freewill, is reason united to faith. Reason is our light, and she explains its efficacy in the realm of the empirical and contingent. Along with Thomas Aquinas (and this is a point to which we shall return) Catherine exalts rather than belittles the value of reason, so that when we transcend the empirical and contingent, faith intervenes to help that

---

[35] Cf. P. Pajardi, *Caterina* ..., cit., pp. 83-84.

[36] Letter 69, to Sano di Maco in Siena: "Here the infinite goodness of God manifests the treasure that he has given to the soul, the treasure of our own free will, that neither the devil nor any creature can ever force to commit a mortal sin if one does not consent to do so" ["*Qui manifesta la smisurata bontà di Dio il tesoro che egli ha dato nell'anima, del proprio e libero arbitrio, che né dimonio né creatura il può costringere a uno peccato mortale, se egli non vuole*"], vol. I, pp. 394-395.

ascent (as Aquinas had said already). She will speak of freedom as "the treasure which God has placed in the soul" [37]and her actions show us that human beings are free, and therefore have a leading role in their own destiny. The soul is free in its choices: "The soul was made out of love and created for love in the image and likeness of God, and cannot exist without love, and it could not love without light. Those who desire to love need to be able to see."[38] Catherine is fanatical about free will, and also about meritocracy.[39] She is convinced about personal and moral freedom, and at the same time, because she experienced this herself, she is convinced about the doctrine of free will. In common with other like-minded thinkers, she loves the theme of personal moral responsibility and existential accountability, of merits and demerits.[40] For her, human beings build their own lives, with the help of divine grace, obviously.

Within the general framework of the development of human personality, Catherine puts the accent on the moment when free will is exercised.[41] This is typically displayed by interventionists, enthusiastic activists, those who are zealous for human intervention in the world's

---

[37] Nothing is more properly ours than free will, which Catherine calls a treasure and Dante calls "The greatest gift that God in his largesse gave to creation, the most attuned to his goodness and that he accounts most dear, was the freedom of the will: all creatures possessed of intellect, all of them and they alone, were and are so endowed" [*lo maggior don che Dio per sua larghezza fesse creando, ed alla sua bontate più conformato, e quel ch'ei più apprezza fu della volontà la libertate di che le creature intelligenti e tutte e sole furon e son dotate."*], *Paradiso*, c.V, v. 19-25.

[38] Letter 113, to Contessa Benedetta daughter of Giovanni d'Agnolino Salimbeni, vol. II, pp. 279-307.

[39] Cf. P. Pajardi, *Caterina* ..., cit., p. 85.

[40] Cf. P. Pajardi, *Caterina* ..., cit., p. 250.

[41] *Dialogue*, part Iª § 2, chap. 14, p. 57: "The soul is like a beautiful vessel disposed to receive grace and for it to grow, little or much, according to how well disposed it wants to be. ... And when it has reached the age of discretion, it will give itself to good or evil according to its pleasure, because of its free will" [*Allora l'anima, come un bel vaso, è disposta a ricevere e aumentare in sé la grazia, poco o molto, secondo che le piacerà di ben disporsi... Quando sarà giunta al tempo della discrezione, potrà darsi al bene o al male, secondo che piacerà alla sua volontà, a cagione del suo libero arbitrio."*]

affairs. Her own life clearly evidenced this, particularly her decision to undertake the journey to Avignon to rouse up the pope.

The freedom God gave to humanity is, in Catherine's way of looking at it, an act of boundless goodness which confers great responsibility. She emphasizes that no-one, nothing, not even the devil can force a creature to sin mortally if that creature does not want it. In her great wisdom she puts into God's mouth this moral assertion: *"I created you without you, but I will not save you without you."* [42]

Comparing the Political Thought of Catherine of Siena and Thomas Aquinas

Catherine's letters reveal how personal dignity is the foundation, security and meaning of political ability. Society, she deduces clearly, has no separate identity, but is composed of the union (*Unitas ordinis*, as St. Thomas Aquinas would say in *Politics* I:1) of individuals, of the creatures who precede and make up society. For St. Catherine, freedom is an essential attribute of the person: "This sweet Father, having created the soul, gives it the treasures of time and free will, to enrich it:"[43] freedom is a condition of the moral life, and is understood not as an absence of limits and obligations but as liberation from the "servitude of sin" and being gifted with the ability to put the good into positive effect.

In Catherine's writings we often find the invitation to "rise above self", to take a place on the seat of conscience and to "take counsel" like a judge in a law court. We are the first judge of ourselves, because the light of reason, strengthened by the light of faith, makes us distinguish between good and evil; we are responsible towards society because our contribution to the common good will vary according to the use made of our freedom. This principle is declared at the very beginning of the *Dialogue*: "The soul cannot be useful to its neighbor if it is not useful to

---

[42] Letter 148, to Pietro Marchese del Monte: "O dear son, we see that God has armed man with a weapon which is so strong that neither demon nor creature can make him offend [God], and this is free will" ["*O carissimo figliuolo, noi vediamo che Dio ha armato l'uomo d'un arma ch'è di tanta fortezza, che né dimonio né creatura il può offendere; e questa è la libera volontà dell'uomo*"], vol. II, p. 410.

[43] Letter 131, to Niccolò Soderini, vol. II, pp. 343-348.

itself first; which means having and acquiring virtue in itself."[44] In our progress towards fulfillment, we have no need of exterior scaffolding, but need to rise on our own foundation as a creature born to love, intelligence and freedom. "God created us free and with power over ourselves."[45]

St. Thomas (to pass to his thought, which Catherine seems mysteriously to echo, and whose studious reflections as a man of faith are very touching) wrote no work in which all principles of social teaching are gathered together organically, because, in the strict sense of the word, he was not political.[46] He left no tract of political science or of social science as we understand it today. Nevertheless, in at least four fundamental books, *Commentaries on Ethics, Aristotle's Politics, De Regimine Principum* and the *Summa Theologiae*, it is possible to deduce his political thought fairly clearly.[47]

In Thomas's conception, politics is *scientia civilis*.[48] It belongs in the domain of practical philosophy, in other words, to "the sector of moral sciences, the sciences of action." In accordance with the long tradition which began with Aristotle, he sees human beings as political and social

---

[44] *Dialogue,* Prologue, chap. 1, pp. 25-26.

[45] Letter 177, to Pietro Cardinale Portuense, vol.III, pp. 117-125.

[46] We find the same idea in E. Flori, *Il trattato 'De regime principum' e le dottrine politiche di S. Tommaso,* Bologna 1927, p. 51; Cf. G. Invitto, *La città dell'uomo. Il pensiero politico di S. Tommaso,* Cavallino di Lecce 1991, p. 13.

[47] Cf. R. Rybka, "L'attuazione del bene comune nel pensiero politico di S.Thomas Aquinas," in *Angelicum,* LXXVII 2000, pp. 477-478.

[48] Thomas Aquinas, in *Libros Politicorum Aristotelis Expositio,* Marietti, Romae, 1951, Prooemium S.Thomae, 5: "*Omnium enim quae ratione cognosci possunt, necesse est aliquam doctrinam tradi ad perfectionem humanae sapientiae quae philosophia vocatur. Cum igitur hoc totum quod est civitas, sit cuidam rationis iudicio subiectum, necesse fuit ad complementum philosophiae de civitate doctrinam tradere quae politica nominatur, idest civilis scientia*", p. 1. ["First, indeed, that we need such knowledge, since we need to teach everything that reason can know for the perfection of human wisdom called philosophy. Therefore, since the whole that is the political community is subject to the judgment of reason, it was necessary for a complete philosophy to give instruction about the political community, instruction called politics (i.e. political science)." Prologue, *Aquinas: Commentary on Aristotle's Politics,* translated by Richard J. Regan, Hackett Publishing Co., 2007), p. 2.]

beings by nature;[49] this principle means that human beings associate together for their needs of their own nature;[50] social and political contacts are innate needs in them.

In other words, we need the essential forms of a life of association to perfect our human nature on all levels; physical, moral and spiritual. Human beings, being "social and political animals" by nature associate together to bring about the common good, which is the goal of their association. Natural sociability in no wise weakens rationality, but rather, works in its favor. Thanks to sociability, each one of us can escape the prison of our own egoism, overcome the erratic movements of our instincts, and move towards the common good of the community in which we live. This natural stimulus towards openness, towards the very purpose of society, guarantees each individual the full realization of their own vocation as a person.[51] In St. Thomas's political thought, true individual good can be achieved only through society.[52] Individual good does not exist unless it is part of the common good. The community's common good has to be realized by all the community and is our common good, the good of each of us. Only thus can it be desired and

---

[49] Thomas Aquinas, *Summa Theologica*, Typis Petri Fiaccadori, Parmae, 1852, I, q. 96, a. 4: "*Primo quidem, quia homo naturaliter est animal sociale: unde homines in statu innocentiae socialiter vixissent*", p. 384 ["First, because man is naturally a social being, and so in the state of innocence he would have led a social life."]

[50] Thomas Aquinas, *De Regimine Principum*, Marietti, Torino, 1948, Liber I, chap.1: "*Naturale autem est homini ut sit animal sociale et politicum in multitudine vivens, magis etiam quam omnia alia animalia, quod quidam naturalis necessitas declarat*", p. 1. ["It is natural to man that he be a social and political animal living among many, more than all other animals, which indeed natural necessity indicates."]

[51] Cf. J. Maritain, *I diritti dell'uomo e la legge naturale*, Milano, 1977, p. 9: "*Il bene comune [...] è la buona vita umana della moltitudine, di una moltitudine di persone, ossia delle totalità carnali e spirituali insieme, e principalmente spirituali, benché accada loro di vivere più sovente nella carne che nello spirit.*" ["The common good...is the good human life of the multitude, of a multitude of persons, that is to say of the totality of flesh and spirit together, but primarily spiritual even if persons happen to live more often in the flesh than in the spirit." Maritain's work in English is *The Rights of Man and Natural Law*.]

[52] Thomas Aquinas, *Summa Contra Gentiles*, Marietti, Romae, 1961, vol. III, Liber III, chap. 117, num. 2894-2900, pp. 175-176.

loved by each individual as my good, and consequently become truly and completely the common good of all.[53]

We can feel Catherine's constant awareness of contemporary events and circumstances in the Church, in the Italian states, in Europe and in the Mediterranean area, at that time exposed to piracy and Turkish invasions. She was imbued with a great sense of responsibility about them; and she believed it was possible, with the help of grace, to preserve the state and reform the Church, for the good of all its citizens.[54]

Catherine's judgment on politics was as follows: "No state can maintain itself in a state of grace with regard to civil law or divine law without holy justice."[55] This statement about the fragility of every human institution separated from grace is the basis of a negative judgment about every political reality that lacks "holy justice." This justice can be the principal informer, healer and perfector of every human activity, even in the political sphere, according to the economy of the relationship between nature and grace, which Thomas famously formulated as "Grace disposes and perfects nature;"[56] a formula which he applied and developed in all his anthropology and which we can sum up in three points:

a) there is a positive relationship between acquired and infused virtues, between ethics and charity, between prudence and wisdom, and, in particular, between the two laws—natural law and divine law—and between political and supernatural cities;[57]

b) there is a moral necessity for divine grace to operate in all fields, even in cultures, common life, politics, in all human wellbeing —everything that orientates human beings towards their true

---

[53] Cf. R. Rybka, *L'attuazione del bene* ..., cit., p. 491.

[54] Cf. R. Spiazzi, *Il Magistero Politico di S. Caterina da Siena nel quadro della tradizione cristiana in confronto con la dottrina di S. Thomas Aquinas*, ed. Cantagalli, Siena, 1972, pp. 3; 6.

[55] *Dialogue*, chap. 119, p. 243.

[56] Thomas Aquinas, *Summa Theologica* ..., cit., I, q. 1, a. 8, ad 2, p. 3.

[57] Cf. *Commentum in quatuor Libros Sententiarum Magistri Petri Lombardi* vol. I, Typis Petri Fiaccadori, Parmae, 1856, III Sent. D. 33, q. 1, a. 4, p. 265; *Summa Theologica* ..., cit., I, q. 98, a.1, ad 3, p. 387.

end;[58]

c) ordered towards this end, all human virtues—and therefore all their activity, even in the political field - have a real value that is both imperfect and perfectible, and which is made fully operational by charity.[59]

Charity, the flowering of grace, is the animating force of civilization, the vivifying breath of the virtue of Law that transforms but not dehumanizes the whole of our life.[60] For St. Thomas, politics is precisely the exercise of "prudence," the virtue that searches out and disposes the means for establishing a just economy of relationships with the desired end.[61] This is the so-called "political prudence" or "governing prudence" which rulers have to exercise, but allcitizens have to have it too, since they contribute or collaborate as conscious and responsible agents in the conduct of public affairs.[62]

Let us go back to St. Paul's reference to prudence: "Be very careful about the sort of lives you lead, like intelligent and not like senseless people" (Eph 5:15), and read what he tells us about what inspires our duties towards society: "And through the grace that I have been given, I say this to every one of you: never pride yourself on being better than you really are, but think of yourself dispassionately, recognizing that God has given to each one his measure of faith. Just as each of us has various parts in one body, and the parts do not all have the same function: in the same way, all of us, though there are so many of us, make up one body in Christ, and as different parts we are all joined to one another. Then since the gifts that we have differ according to the grace that was given to each of us: if it is a gift of prophecy, we should prophesy as much as our faith tells us; if it is a gift of practical service, let us devote ourselves to serving; if it is teaching, to teaching; if it is encouraging, to encouraging. When you give, you should give generously from the heart; if you are put in charge, you must be conscientious; if you do works of mercy, let it be

---

[58] Thomas Aquinas, *Summa Theologica* ..., cit., II, q. 109 spec. aa. 2, 4, 8, pp. 429; 431; 434.

[59] Thomas Aquinas, *Summa Theologica* ..., cit., I, q. 65, a. 2, pp. 235-236.

[60] Cf. R. Spiazzi, *Il Magistero* ..., cit., p. 7.

[61] Thomas Aquinas, *Summa Theologica* ..., cit., I, q. 47, aa. 1-2, pp. 193-194.

[62] Thomas Aquinas, *Summa Theologica* ..., cit., II, q. 50, a. 2, pp. 204-205.

because you enjoy doing them" (Rm 12: 3-8). Catherine has "discretion" as the keystone of all her ethical and ascetic teaching; it is the essence but not the equivalent of prudence.[63] For her, as for St. Thomas, it was a faculty of judgment dictated interiorly, by which we are kept steadily on the path of justice.[64]

This is her summons: "...I have desired to see you in the most perfect charity...and with the light of discretion to be able to give yourself to each one...." [65] To Andrea di Vanni: "..Just as the perfect love of God generates perfect love of neighbor, so should it be with the perfection with which a man rules himself and rules his subjects...I have desired to see you a just and true governor."[66] But prudence, that is, discretion, says Catherine, applies to that "sweet and true awareness" which is conscience; so that there are no good "Christian politics", or even good human politics, if there is not a right and just conscience: which means being explicitly and substantially a disciple of truth.[67]

Realistic and Current Thinking

A gathering of specific points and basic texts from Catherine's works will give us her social philosophy: "In this mortal life, while you are still pilgrims, I have bound you together with the chain of charity: whether you want it or not, you are so bound. If the affection of your charity towards your neighbor diminishes, you are still bound to them by need. I desire that you exercise charity either in the affection of the heart or in

---

[63] *Dialogue*, chap. 9: *"Discrezione non è altro che una vera conoscenza che l'anima deve avere di sé e di me. In questa conoscenza la discrezione tiene fisse le sue radici. Ella è come un rampollo, innestato e unito con la carità"*, pp. 43-44 ["Discretion is nothing other than a true knowledge that the soul must have of itself and of Me, and in this knowledge virtue is rooted. Discretion is the only child of self-knowledge and, when espoused to charity, has many other offspring..."].

[64] Thomas Aquinas, *Summa Theologica* ..., cit., I, q. 79, a.13, pp. 317-318; I, q. 14, aa. 3, 5, pp. 60-63; I, q. 47, aa. 2, 6, 7, pp. 193-195.

[65] Letter 33, to the Abbot of the Order of Monte Oliveto in the contado of Siena, vol. I, pp. 183-189.

[66] Letter 358, to Maestro Andrea di Vanni, *Capitano* of the people of Siena vol. V, pp. 232-237.

[67] Cf. R. Spiazzi: *Il Magistero* ..., cit., p. 8.

at least in external actions, so that even if your affection wanes, because of your sinfulness, you are at least constrained by your very needs to perform these acts. I have not given to any one person to know all that is needed for human life; but to one a part, to another a part, so that if one is in need he goes to the other. In this way, the artisan goes to the laborer, the laborer to the artisan; each has need of the other, because he does not know how to do what the other is doing. It is like that in everything."[68]

- "Every creature gifted with reason has a vineyard within, the vineyard of the soul; throughout life free will labors there. When this life is ended, no one can labor, either for good or for ill, whereas while alive, all can labor in the vineyard where I have placed them."[69]
- "Positions of authority are lent, for a time ...according to the ways and customs of the country, they pass from us, for good or for ill."[70]
- All who have been "lent" positions of authority must put themselves entirely at the service of the subjects,[71] and their actions must be inspired by "holy justice and true humility."[72] To command is to be seen as a privilege to serve, rather than a power. Obedience to legitimate authority is seen as an act of justice."

Her letters sometimes inspire, sometimes exhort: "Love each other; if you do evil among yourselves, there will be no one who will do good to

[68] *Dialogue*, chap. 148, pp. 330-331. Note the consonance of this passage with St. Thomas Aquinas in II-II, q. 40, a. 2.

[69] *Dialogue*, chap. 23, pp. 65-66.

[70] Letter 123, to the *Signori difensori* [Lord defenders] of the city of Siena, vol. II, p. 303.

[71] Letter 96, to Pietro Canigiani in Firenze, vol. I, pp.142-150; Letter 357, to the king of Hungary, vol. V, pp. 222-232.

[72] Letter 149, to Messer Pietro Gambacorti in Pisa, vol. II, pp. 415-419; Letter 372, to Messer Carlo della Pace, who was then king of Puglia or Naples, vol. V, pp. 303-311.

you;"[73] "The soul cannot be useful to its neighbor if it is not first useful to itself by having and acquiring virtue;"[74] "If we do not correct ourselves while we have the time, the shining pearl of holy justice is put out, and the warmth of true charity and obedience is lost."[75]

Catherine was always reminding statesmen and pastors of the Church about their responsibility to govern, and about their task to make justice triumph.[76] This teaching, this call, was made to everyone, beginning with Pope Gregory XI, whom she did not hesitate to remind that if he had taken authority he must use it: "I have long desired to see you a strong man and fearless."[77] Justice as a virtue is something interior, putting a person into total inward rather than exterior order. "If a man has been given authority to govern others, he has to rule and govern himself first. How can a blind man see and guide others?"[78]

In Letter 268, she raises a close and rigorous criticism of politics that are dominated by self-love and rooted in injustice; this criticism finds its logical conclusion in the demand for truth which is the foundation of justice and the key to the common good. To achieve self-mastery in the love of God, the three interior powers have to be put into action: memory, intellect and will; having achieved this order, a man is capable of governing others. This is the principle and criterion for applying this to political action, taking note of the complexity of the various situations in which there is need to work. Peace, too, as the state's reason for being, enters into the new balance of the virtues, and is the fruit of charity.[79] Catherine shares the thomistic conception of peace as the end and also the condition of civilization; the state has to ensure and promote it; she

---

[73] Letter 377 [Gardner IV], to the *Signori Priori dell'Arti* [Lord Priors of the Arts] and to the *Gonfaloniere della Giustizia* [the Standard-bearer of Justice] of Florence, vol. V, pp. 336-341.

[74] *Dialogue*, Prologue, chap. I, p. 26.

[75] Letter 268, to the *Anziani* and *Consoli* and *Gonfalonieri* of Bologna, vol. IV, pp. 160-166.

[76] Cf. R. Spiazzi, *Il Magistero* ..., cit., p. 16.

[77] Letter 270, to Gregorio XI, vol. IV, p. 168.

[78] Letter 121, to the *Signori Difensori*, and *Capitano* of the People of Siena, at Sant'Antimo, vol. II, p. 279.

[79] Cf. R. Spiazzi, *Il Magistero* ..., cit., pp. 19-22.

will not countenance weakness and encourages the use of might to defend the population from injustice or the Church from division, even by a crusade, if necessary. "In this life we are posted as in a battle camp, and have to fight manfully and not avoid blows or turn our heads away, but keep our gaze on our captain, Christ Crucified."[80]

Today, without "confessionalism" but with the vigor of an enlightened and fearless conscience, Catherine teaches all of us, even politicians, that charity is not only the central value of Christian ethics but also the unfailing source of true civilization.[81] She had, as we have seen, a thomistic formation and her fundamental conception of social doctrine was based on the dignity of the human person. Human society can have no other connective tissue than charity, a charity that obviously goes far beyond an existentially necessary solidarity. Nothing if not realistic, Catherine criticizes humanity as a figure whose ideas are essentially feeble, a mere hanging on to the status quo.[82]

The common good of society concerns much more than the administration and use of exclusively temporal and material goods; it concerns the end or purpose of human life, and the complex goals of its very existence. It seems important, therefore, to state that Catherine identifies justice as source and foundation of the common good.

She teaches us that justice ensures both the common and individual good. So where there is injustice, there can only be social disorder and serious danger to the individual who believes that happiness can be gained through a disordered quest for a particular great good. "I, Catherine am writing to you...with the desire to see the light of holy justice in your heart, lifting you out of all self-love and attentive to the universal good of your city, not to your own particular good."[83] Individual justice too must be coordinated with universal justice, because the virtuc is one and the same, unifying just as charity does;[84] if

---

[80] Letter 159, to Frate Ranieri of the Dominican Church of Santa Caterina in Pisa, vol. III, p. 27.

[81] Cf. R. Spiazzi, *Il Magistero ...*, cit., p. 25.

[82] Cf. P. Pajardi, *Caterina ...*, cit., pp. 111-112.

[83] Letter 367, to the *Magnifici Signori Difensori* of the people of the commune of Siena, vol. V, p. 279.

[84] Cf. P. Pajardi, *Caterina ...*, cit., pp. 13-14.

an individual suffers injustice, all society suffers it, and the common good suffers too. In reality, this conceals the personal interests of the holders of power, who evade the duty of service and selfishly appropriate to themselves the functions which society has entrusted to them solely for collective interests. "There are others who hold their heads high because of the power they wield: and this power shows all the signs of injustice, injustice committed towards God, towards neighbor and towards themselves."[85]

All Catherine's public activity (and this shows her universality and particularly how she kept in touch with current affairs) aimed at calling people to change, to a radical inward transformation. She showed that she had little confidence in modifying or ordering systems; she tried to make breaches in minds and hearts. For her, politics found its justification and its limits in the ordering of the human person; she stated that society is at the service of the individual, not the other way round, which is a clear thomistic conception of the subsidiarity of what is public to what is private.[86]

Human destiny is at stake, and to be committed to politics is, for man, a duty; the social dimension is as much a part of being human as the individual dimension. Certainly, politics is a means, not an end; and it is a part, not the whole. The earthly city is not the private possession of the one who governs it; it is a "lent" city, which Catherine also tells us in her letters: "He who rules, possesses his authority in holy fear, with ordered, not disordered love; as a thing that is lent, not as his own property."[87] This is the meaning of mandate, from which the meaning of service is derived. The one who can do more, should do more; the more authority, the more duties.

"There are three fundamental sins for the politician and the public administrator: to avoid the contest, to delay decisions, and to tolerate evil."[88] These sins she sums up as "the sleep of negligence." The thought

---

[85] *Dialogue*, chap. 34, p. 84.

[86] Cf. P. Pajardi, *Caterina* ..., cit., pp. 117-118.

[87] Letter 123, to the *Signori difensori* of the city of Siena, vol. II, pp. 304f.

[88] Letter 123, to the *Signori difensori* of the city of Siena, vol. II, pp. 304f.

expressed in her letters is, "the one who does not know how to govern himself cannot govern others."[89]

This was the context in which Catherine, with thomistic lucidity, placed the relationship between the individual and society; for her the key to freedom and authority was the exercise of power. It is clear that authority must not abuse freedom; on the contrary, the citizen cannot withdraw himself from observing the laws and from obedience to the governor, if authority is exercised well, and power is administered correctly, even when part of his freedom needs to be sacrificed for the common good when necessary. This "submission" is understood as an act of individual and social justice, without which authority is wasted and chaos reigns.

The meaning of power as service: politics as the complex administration of human affairs from the point of view of civil government of society are presented as the indispensible condition for raising human dignity, in providing the means for the best possible way of living, in encouraging freedom, in guaranteeing justice in human relationships, in order to make this world the best possible place.[90]

Catherine does not exclude divergence of opinions, ideological or cultural pluralism, or what we today would call party politics: she preaches tolerance, substantial unity, the ability to overcome divisions in order to find common ground. We may imagine her as a strong and lofty personage who points her finger at governors,[91] not to accuse them but to exhort them to understand and remember an essential idea – the "city," that is, civic power, is not given them for themselves; it is lent to them in order that they can govern well, and exercise power correctly, in service to those whom they govern. It is not to enrich them, but to enable them to be responsible. Human beings are nothing in themselves and possess nothing, everything is there so that it can grow, and it grows by self-realization.[92] The path to action leads from ideas: action in itself has

---

[89] Letter n.121, to the *Signori Difensori*, and *Capitano* of the People of the city of Siena, being at Sant'Antimo, vol. II, p. 279.

[90] Cf. P. Pajardi, *Caterina ...*, cit., pp. 125-126.

[91] Cf. P. Pajardi, *Caterina ...*, cit., pp. 148.

[92] Letter 68, vol. I, p. 381; Letter 116, vol. II, p. 257; Letter 123, vol. II, p. 297; Letter 171, vol. III, p. 85.

no value so the passage is towards action; action itself is not a value, but action in as far as it brings us towards an end, operating in a close cooperation of mind, soul and heart to affect the external world through the instrument of the will.[93]

A social philosophy

Human beings have needs and desires and Catherine deeply understood this; these needs are more than economic ones, and they have to be more than just political. Human beings are unique; they have their own dignity, reason and essential freedom. They need existential reasons, orientation for their freedom, and values which enable them to transcend themselves.[94]

Precisely because we are free, we are called to assume responsibilities, which on one hand derive from being incorporated into civil life as a moral subject, capable of distinguishing positive from negative, and which, on the other hand, are derived from professional commitments. The meaning and dignity of human life are closely connected with acting responsibly, and Catherine makes constant reference to this.

To go more deeply into this introductory picture, we turn our attention to a critical analysis of our own times, and on how *justice* is to be understood.

With the loss, at a social and political level, of a common vision of the good, what we have left is a collection of individuals with particular (even discordant) interests, whose living together is guaranteed by a system of practical rules. In practice, justice, no longer having any reference to what is *good*, has lost its role of virtue and is identified with a system of subjective laws which are aimed at assuring our ability to live together. To be *just* does not mean giving each what they need to realise their essential role as citizens; it means, rather, to limit oneself to a formal and juridical respect of the common rules of life. It follows that, on one hand, the good is no longer understood as a complex and

---

[93] Cf. P. Pajardi, *Caterina ...*, cit., p. 158.

[94] Cf. A. Lobato, 1992: *Europa unita, utopia o realtà? La Filosofia risponde, in Filosofia e cultura nell'Europa di domani,* B. Mondin (ed.), Città Nuova Ed., Roma, 1993, pp. 124-125.

objectively sensible need; it leaves the area of morality and becomes a fulcrum for subjective interests and individual happiness. And justice, instead of being a cultural value in social life and human cooperation, has become the realm of impartiality and moral legalities.[95]

It is in this sense that the concentration on modern and contemporary ethics is explained. The fundamental moral question concentrates on what I have the *duty* to do in relation to others, and completely bypasses the eudemonistic (happiness through virtue) problem of free and responsible moral formation in itself, considering it bound up with subjective and experiential factors.

On the contrary; it belongs to the virtue of justice to recognise that both I and others have equal claims to a good life. It follows that there cannot be a good life for me if there is not a good life for others: justice has to be found in a universal good.[96]

This is how Catherine's model of government works out in practice; a governor should be interventionist but reflective, prudent, resolute, firm and consistent. One who does not hesitate or delay, one with pure morals, generous in offering personal energies for a cause; one who is intent only on the common good. One whose actions, and whose sturdy, reliable character, are underpinned by truth, justice and good spirit; by the avoidance of all personal self-interest, of all illicit and wicked private interests; one who is fearless and does not hope for personal gain. Be humble, says the saint to those who govern. "Govern yourselves first, because if you do not learn to govern your own life properly, you cannot claim to order the lives of others."[97]

"Do everything according to right reason, in the light of faith, and in the spirit of charity, so that justice's rule, 'to each what belongs to them' will give each one the prospect of highest respect and recognition. Once your rightly and fully informed conscience is tranquil, have no fear of anyone's dissent: because it is better to be just while appearing to be unjust than to be unjust while appearing to be just; and do not despise

---

[95] Cf. M. Matteini, *Macintyre e la rifondazione dell'etica*, Città Nuova Ed., Roma, 1995, p. 97.

[96] Cf. M. Matteini, *Macintyre e la ...*, cit., p. 96.

[97] Letter 121, to the *Signori Difensori* and *Capitano* of the people of the city of Siena at Sant'Antimo, vol. II, p. 279.

the tribulations that can follow on your right conduct. Live in the spirit of truth, for it will season all the virtues and keep them bright with the light of truth."[98]

In the search for freedom and full political involvement, her thought will help us in the meaningful and fascinating recovery of the common roots of our western moral patrimony. There is an interesting space between our "narration" and the norms closely linked to particular traditions, and it is an open way to a new universality. It is a space where particular categories like those of human rights or the rights of the natural world, or of virtue, can operate with creativity.[99]

In Catherine's mind and soul, there was a real sense of the concrete, the real and the contingent. This made her suffer terribly, like any idealist who discovers an immense distance between the real and the ideal, and realizes what great labor lies ahead to bring the real up to the level of the ideal.

The character of political personalities is measured by the greatness of their plans and the complexity of their actions; this was particularly true of Catherine, all the more because of the discordant and complicated outlook of the vast European political scenario of those days. It is precisely here that she had a decisive effect as an element of harmony and equilibrium.

Through her experience of life she gives us a penetrating theo-logical teaching, a fascinating ontology, and, at the same time, a prophetic social and political doctrine. She draws our attention, and that of personalities of her own time, to true discernment. Her anthropology is concerned with human values and human rights.

Her witness and her teaching are aimed at drawing us towards the truth operative within us, and towards the freedom that is its explicit expression. She is quite clear that the goal of society is the "universal common good," to which the "particular good" must be subordinated. The common good, which guarantees the good of each individual, depends, she says, on "holy and real justice." This "pearl must shine

---

[98] Cf. P. Pajardi, *Caterina...*, cit., pp. 206-207.

[99] Cf. Teodora Rossi, *"Natura, Ratio, Ordo. Rilettura all'interno del discorso morale attuale,"* in *Angelicum* LXXII 1995, p. 384.

again" in the regulation of public affairs, so that each one "may be given what is due."[100] She points out three necessary conditions for good government:[101]

- awareness that government is "something lent, not possessed";[102]
- rulers must uphold "holy and true justice" to keep the city or state in peace;[103]
- delight in and love of one's neighbour.

She reminds us that "to rule others" demands that we first rule ourselves, because "the one who does not know how to govern himself, cannot govern others." She considers that the one who governs has a duty to exercise, and allow others to exercise, the gift of freedom. The precious foundation for all this is "free will," which guides the three powers of the soul—memory, understanding and will—towards that which is loved.[104] Human beings will be truly free, therefore, even politically, when these three powers can express themselves to the full.

Philosophical inspiration, which is necessarily immersed in historical vision, is arousing a theological vision aimed at recovering moral orientation and political identity. We are seeing a re-foundation of ethics based on the teachings of Catherine of Siena, who in her turn was inspired by the teaching of the illustrious Dominican theologian and philosopher Thomas Aquinas. Her teaching is capable of having an immediate effect on social issues. This takes us, necessarily, towards an anthropological vision eminently suitable for redeeming and re-evaluating the Aristotelian "social animal," whose freedom and essence is found in being a complete person: "an individual who is rational by

---

[100] Letter 311, to the *Signori Difensori* to the people and commune of Siena, vol. IV, pp. 382-389.

[101] Letter 235, vol. III, pp. 421-428, to the king of France.

[102] Letter 123, vol. II, pp. 297-307, to the *Signori difensori* of the city of Siena.

[103] Letter 350, vol. V, pp. 172-181, , to the king of France; Letter 24 vol. I, pp. 120-126, to Biringhieri degli Arzocchi, parish priest of Asciano.

[104] Letter 313, vol. IV, pp. 399-409, to the count of Fondi.

nature"[105] and who, through will and understanding, manifests an authentic and original humanity.

To recognise the enormous importance that an analysis of our rational and political nature has for ethics, leads to the concept being developed not only for the logical consistency of single actions; it also gives a moral profile of human beings as executors of their own deeds, and responsible for their essential goals, continually committed to human and moral perfection.

This is the most important teaching Catherine has left us.

---

[105] Thomas Aquinas, *Summa Theologica*, I, q. 29, a. 1, pp. 124-125.

4

The Holy Spirit in the Prayers of St. Catherine of Siena

Yves Congar, O.P.

Having just completed the edition of three volumes on the Holy Spirit, I decided to celebrate the sixth centenary of the death of St. Catherine by examining the place of the Holy Spirit, admittedly not in her life and in all her writings, but rather in her prayers.[1] I admit I was a little puzzled by the style of her prayers. They are incredibly dogmatic. Granted, there is a profound bond and connection between doxology and theology. In naming God and in praising him, in detailing his greatness and generosity, we outline the foundations of dogmatic theology. Think, for example, of the first fourteen verses of the letter to the Ephesians. But for Catherine it is not a case of doxology pregnant with theology, but rather of a theology that is transformed into doxology. It is the *sacra doctrina* become fire and fervor. It is precisely the Holy Spirit within this fire and fervor in the soul, who is the minister guaranteeing the role of the doctrine in nourishing the soul.[2]

---

[1] S. Caterina da Siena, *Le orazioni,* ed. and trans. Giuliana Cavallini (Roma: Edizioni Cateriniane, 1978). [For an English translation of the prayers, cf. Catherine of Siena, *The Prayers of Catherine of Siena,* 2nd ed. and trans. Suzanne Noffke, OP (San Jose: Authors Choice Press, 2001). There are various numbering systems for Catherine's letters and prayers. In this article the Roman numerals indicate the number of the prayer in Cavallini's edition; the arabic numerals indicate the number of the prayer in Noffke's translation. Thus, XXIV/5 means prayer XXIV in Cavallini and prayer 5 in Noffke. - Ed.]

[2] See Prayer XXII/12. "...the Holy Spirit is indeed a servant for us."

This prayed theology is fundamentally trinitarian.[3] The Trinity is the ineffable Godhead in its totality. Catherine constantly entwines the attributes proper to, or attributed to, each of the Persons, and their image and effect in us.

> Power of the eternal Father, help me; wisdom of the Son, illumine the eye of my intellect; sweet clemency of the Holy Spirit, inflame and unite my heart in you. (Prayer XXIV/5)

With the same constancy found in her Letters, power is attributed to the Father, wisdom to the Son, and clemency or the will and goodness to the Holy Spirit.[4] God is love; God is "in love". Is it because Catherine sees everything under the guise of love that the Trinity is a gushing forth of love? It is remarkable that the Father, or the Godhead, are often designated as uncreated Love, Creator through love.[5]

This Trinitarian vision of God is reflected in his image in human beings. Catherine tirelessly expresses in the Prayers, *Dialogue* and Letters, the theology and anthropology of what we call the psychological Trinity.[6] It is impossible that she did not have some familiarity with St. Augustine, whether through St. Thomas, not to mention St. Bernard or St. Bonaventure;[7] not through her own reading, since she did not learn to read until later in life, and then only modestly (the breviary), but through her directors: William of Flete or Alfonso de Vadaterra, two Augustinian hermits, and through her own friends, the Friars Preachers.

---

[3] Fr. Alvaro Grion, OP, began his fine study *Santa Caterina, Dottrina e Fonti* (Brescia: Morcelliana, 1953) with the Trinity.

[4] See the letters in Grion, pp. 175 and 176 note 1. The same author notes on page 226 that this is not found in Ubertino da Casale, one of Catherine's sources. [The noted Catherinian scholar Giacinto D'Urso, O.P., strongly disagrees that Ubertino is one of Catherine's sources. For his review of Grion's work, cf. "Il pensiero di S. Caterina e le sue fonti," *Sapienza*, VIII, 1954, n. 305, pp. 335-388. The article was reprinted in D'Urso, *Il genio di Santa Caterina*. Quaderni Cateriniani no. 8 (Roma: Edizioni Cateriniane, 1971), pp. 90-192. –Ed.]

[5] Cf. Prayers IV/13; V/7; XI/18; XVIII/24, "O Deity, love-Deity"; XIX/9; XX/10, "O Trinity eternal, O fire and abyss of charity...O eternal fire"; XXII/12.

[6] For the *Dialogue and Letters*, the references are in Grion, p. 22 note 3. Note also in Grion, p. 228, where Ubertino da Casale is not a source for Catherine.

[7] St. Bernard, *In Cant.* XI, 5-6; St. Bonaventure, *Soliloq.*, prol. 3; I, 3.

I would be inclined to see a sign that this Trinitarian theological anthropology may be more thomistic, however, in the fact that the theme of the Holy Spirit as the bond of love between the Father and the Son is very rarely found—only once, if I am not mistaken: XXIII/4 —while the theme of the image is constant. The Love-Deity has, through love, created humankind in his image and likeness; he has given him "the form of the Trinity" in the powers of the soul: in the image of the Father—the memory that sustains and protects; the intelligence; and finally, the will, the sweet clemency of the Holy Spirit.[8] Catherine is deliberate. For her the Spirit is love, the efficacious movement of the will; she compares it to the hand that executes what the mind conceives.[9] However, Catherine is particularly fond of two comparisons, which although they are different, are intermingled in Prayer V/7, that of fire and that of the germination of beautiful plants in a garden, *giardino*, or an orchard, *viridarium*.

The Holy Spirit is a fire that burns and thus purifies hearts of their carnal affections. He is the fire and the abyss of love that sustained Christ affixed to the cross (XXIV/5).[10] He is also a fire that illuminates and warms, since he is in God, Love, eternal Fire.[11] St. Paul united his will perfectly to the Holy Spirit by loving the Love and Clemency that he is, and in virtue of which we exist (XXIII/4). Catherine is very fond of the theme of enlightenment through knowledge. The Spirit guarantees this service of enlightening the eye of our intellect by inspiring it to follow the teaching of the Lamb who gives himself as nourishment at the twin tables of the Word and the Sacrament.[12]

In Prayer V/7, uttered December 21, 1378, Catherine moves on from the idea of the Fire of the Holy Spirit, which must consume and root out the carnal affections of the heart of the new plants, to the theme which is

---

[8] Prayers I/1; XIII/20; XVI/23; XVII/22; XXI/11; XXIII/4.

[9] Prayer I/1; in a note, G. Cavallini refers to Letters 129 and 183. In Prayer XI/18, the Spirit is the hand with which God wrote the Trinity in Mary, forming within her the Incarnate Word.

[10] Prayers V/7; XX/10. Compare with XXIV/5 ("inflame and unite hearts to the goodness of God").

[11] Prayer XIV/25 (January 1, 1378)

[12] Prayer XXII/12; for the Spirit is the servant, serving at the table when the Son of the Father is given as food. G. Cavallini refers to the *Dialogue* LXXVIII. Cf. also Grion, p. 131 note 1.

dear to her, that of a garden or orchard where plants flower and bear fruit, according to the heart of God. Prayer and imagery reflect a very concrete event: the nomination of the new cardinals by Urban VI, September 1378.[13] The image of the garden or orchard is dear to Catherine. She translates the concept of fecundity, and covers the entire economy of grace, which flows into souls from the heart of God who is Love, and creates the Mystical Body, which for Catherine, is the Roman Church.

> In the garden of your bosom, Eternal Father, the human person was enclosed:
> You have drawn him from your holy mind, like a flower petaled into the three powers of the soul....(Prayer XIII/20)

God is a tree of life who has drawn from himself the tree of his creature with its branches, which are the powers of the soul: intelligence, memory and will; in the latter is the fruit of love.[14] This refers to persons, but Catherine has the Church in view. Catherine arrived in Rome when the papal schism was over. She thus beseeches God on February 13, 1379:

> O inestimable and sweetest charity, this is your garden, founded on your blood and watered with the blood of your martyrs who ran bravely after the fragrance of your blood. You, then, be the one to guard it. For who is the one who could prevail against the city that you would protect? Set our hearts ablaze... (Prayer XIX/9).

Catherine would like to join the martyrs and shed her blood in the sacred garden. A few days later, February 2, she prays thus:

---

[13] See Cavallini's comments on pp. 49 and 54 note 16 in S. Caterina da Siena, *Le orazioni* (1978). In Letter 291, Catherine writes: "reform again the garden of your Bride with good and virtuous plants; carefully choosing a company of the holiest men...And not those who are looking for greatness but who are shepherds who with solicitude will govern their flock. And a company of good cardinals who will be for you solid pillars of support."

[14] Prayer X/17; in note 1 on p. 106 of *Le orazioni* (1978), Cavallini cites parallels in the *Dialogue.* In Prayer XIII/20 Catherine says that God gave to man and woman intelligence to understand the truth and his will so as to bring forth in us the flower of glory to his name, the fruit of virtue, and holiness.

> Turn, turn, merciful Father, the eye of your pity on your Bride
> and on your Vicar; hide him under the wings of your mercy so
> that the malice of the proud may not hurt him, and grant to me
> grace to shed my blood and spread the marrow of my bones in
> this garden of holy Church. (Prayer VIII/15)

Thus, in her prayer as in her action, the mystical and the political are
entwined. The political is the cardinals' support for Urban VI, and also
the "Servants of God", the holy souls, especially the hermits, with whom
Catherine wanted to surround the Pope. It is also the intense
propaganda, even advice about the Crusade which Catherine had
generously provided in Urban's favor. The mystical is the sacrifice of
blood, the ardent pleading, the invocation of the Holy Spirit in a letter
dated, undoubtedly, to May 1379, and addressed to Urban VI:

> Most Holy Father, may the Holy Spirit overshadow your soul
> and your heart and your affection with the fire of divine
> charity, and pour a supernatural light into your intellect (...) I
> hope that this sweet fire of the Holy Spirit will work in your
> heart and in your soul as it did in those holy disciples when it
> gave them fortitude and power against demons visible [the
> partisans of the anti-Pope Clement VII] and invisible.[15]

The Holy Spirit is here especially as a Spirit of power. It is a matter of
encouraging the Pope.

Obviously, Catherine knows what spiritual combat is. God is the good
tree but there is also a tree of evil, a tree of death (cf. note 14).
Uncircumcised hearts resist the Holy Spirit who knocks at the door of
these souls. Catherine prays that they may be enlightened (XIV/25). I
want to comment on this subject. I was astonished not to encounter a
reference to the gifts of the Holy Spirit in the Prayers. I am not sure what
the situation is in the *Dialogue* and the Letters. The fact is a little
astonishing when we think of the role that the gifts play in the theology
of St. Thomas. It seems that Catherine does not like to itemize spiritual
realities. We have noted that, for her, Faith encompasses everything.
Perhaps for her also, the Holy Spirit is *the* gift. Subsequent to her prayer
of December 21, 1378, for the new plants in the garden of the Church—

---

[15] Letter 351, *Le Lettere di S. Caterina da Siena*...a cura di Piero Misciattelli,
vol. V, 2nd ed. (Siena, 1913), p. 234.

this refers to the new cardinals and papal assistants —Catherine begs that they have a pure heart, that they assist the Vicar of Christ, that they grow as examples of holy and moral character, and that they bring forth sweet-smelling flowers and delicious fruits. Finally, I quote:

> Cut off the movements of all carnal affection with your celestial gift with which you bathed the holy apostles in the dew of the Holy Spirit.... (Prayer V/7)

The gift is that of the dew of the Holy Spirit. We know that for St. Augustine and for St. Thomas, the title "Gift", along with that of "Love", is a proper name of the Holy Spirit. In the liturgy too, we sing in the *Veni Creator*, "Gift of God most high".

Nowhere does Catherine invoke the Spirit as an independent force that would push her to actions "prophetic" or extraordinarily "inspired". It is possible that in the rumors and suspicions of which she was the object, and which led her to a hearing before the General Chapter of 1374, that she may have been suspected of latent Joachinism. What mystic was not so accused? Nothing is more alien to her. While some investigations produce sufficient evidence, the references to the Holy Spirit that we find in her Letters are very few. Either they are very classic invitations not to resist the Holy Spirit,[16] or else they aim to enliven the understanding and the message of the preacher.[17] With Catherine, the Holy Spirit is always understood in a rigorous Trinitarian theology. Her church is the Mystical Body of Christ, and this Mystical Body is the Roman Church with its priests, its Pope, and its sacraments. Catherine's inspiration is totally in union with the institutional Church. It is she, the Church, that must be God's garden which the Spirit purifies and where he causes the plants, sweet-smelling and laden with fruit, to grow.

We have, however, left aside Prayer XXV/6—and it is the only one addressed to the Holy Spirit. Fr. Alvaro Grion rejects it as non-catherinian by reason of its content.[18] As a matter of fact, she invokes

---

[16] See for example Letter 198 to Fra Bartolomeo Dominici (pub. note 15, vol. III, 1913, p. 207) or Letter 200 in the same work p. 126.

[17] Thus Letter 205 to Stefano di Corrado Maconi; Letter 206 to Gregory XI.

[18] Grion, note 3, pp. 174-177. Cavallini, on the contrary, considers the authenticity of the prayer as possible. See *Le orazioni* (1978), pp. 276-277.

the Holy Spirit under the title of power ("through your power..."), while, without exception with Catherine, power is attributed to the Father and clemency to the Spirit. We are far too incompetent to judge the cogent character of this reasoning. To tell the truth, we distrust restrictions that one would impose on a spiritual activity in the name of rigid coherence. But this prayer is relatively commonplace and adds nothing to our research. Let us merely note, in view of our general interest in pneumatology that once more a prayer addressed to the Holy Spirit begins with the invitation "Come"![19]

---

[19] Cf. Congar's *Je crois en l'Esprit-Saint,* vol. I, pp. 155-157; vol. II, pp. 147-148 (Paris, both 1979). Translation: *I Believe in the Holy Spirit,* trans. David Smith (London: Geoffrey Chapman, 1983), Vol. I, 108-111 and Vol. II, 112. (Three volumes in one).

5

Processo Castellano
An Excerpt from the Testimony
of Fra Bartolomeo Dominici

Michael J. Houser

Introduction:

An original process of certain sayings and attestations concerning the celebrated memory and the virtues, life, and doctrine of blessed Catherine of Siena, which were publicly brought forward in the episcopal curia of Castello di Venezia at different times mentioned below and deposed by certain below-mentioned venerable religious fathers of diverse orders, ranks, and places, who are of commendable life, knowledge, and reputation. This original process, by command of the reverend father and lord Francesco Bembo, bishop of Castello di Venezia by the grace of God and the Apostolic See, was published, written, and placed in the chancery of the aforesaid curia by me, Francesco da Viviano, notary of the said episcopal curia. I also wrote, authenticated, and published this process with my own hand, and confirmed it with my accustomed sign and name, as is evident throughout the whole course of this process, and especially at the end.

Fra Bartolomeo Dominici

Concerning the prologue of the matters written below, in which mention is made of three defects of the above-mentioned declarations and of the provision for them by the witness

    I.   through certain additions against the first defect,
    II. through certain declarations against the second defect,
    III. and through certain complementary narrations to be made against the third.

To the Venerable Padre Fra Thomas.

When recently, that is, in the month of October 1412, I had transmitted to your reverence certain attestations of mine, redacted in a public form, with the signature of two notaries and of my hand, and with the impression of my seal, making mention of the sanctity of life and truth of doctrine of the Blessed Catherine of Siena, immediately afterwards, as my conscience was troubling me, I realized that I had omitted many things that needed to be recounted, and had not transmitted to you a finished narration but, as it were, a truncated one, for which reason I then and there, full of shame, was sorrowful, and decided in my mind to emend the aforesaid defects. However, not many days after, I received your many letters in succession, in which you make mention that you had discovered that in my aforesaid attestations were many defects, namely the two already mentioned by me, adding that in certain points my aforementioned attestations seemed to contradict the ordinary *Legenda* on those same points.

I

Concerning the completion and addition to the above-mentioned declarations against the first defect:

- and first, telling of the virgin's marvelous manner of living and her miraculous fast of fifty days without any food and drink;
- second, telling of the marvelous manner of reception by the virgin both of the Host, and of the wine from the chalice after her sacramental communion[1];
- third, telling of the wondrous manner of sacramental confession which was made to him by the virgin;
- fourth, telling of the wondrous efficacy of the virgin for converting, knowing, and drawing to herself souls of any sex, condition and state and similarly with regard to those who envied her, making explicit mention of some;
- fifth, telling of the wondrous response made by the virgin when he [Fra Bartolomeo] rebuked her because she was seen to accept the honors and reverences made to her; and

---

[1] It was customary in many places in the Middle Ages for the faithful to be given unconsecrated wine to drink as an ablution after the reception of Holy Communion under the species of bread alone.

- sixth, telling of the remarkable response of the virgin to a certain letter in the manner of a correction which had been sent to her by a certain servant of God.

Beginning, therefore, from the first, since plainly you say that my aforesaid attestations are too diminished, especially since I in the prologue of them said that I knew more about the things pertaining to the praise and glory of the said holy memory of Catherine of Siena than anyone else alive in body. As far as this is concerned, I confess that I was silent about many things on purpose, just as I said beforehand, in the prologue of those things, that I would be; and this for the purpose of avoiding excessive length. Also, in the second chapter of the aforesaid attestations, I made special mention of certain things which for the sake of brevity I was intending to omit, things which, extensively and truthfully, the ordinary *Legenda* treats of cautiously and devoutly: by which words of mine, it seems to me, I confirm that all the things are true which are told in that ordinary *Legenda,* which I specifically say that I want to pass over: and thus, in a certain way, I narrate all those things about which in the aforesaid chapter I make brief and succinct mention.

FIRST

However, so that I might somehow supply this defect, I will add the narration of certain other things to these; and since in the your aforesaid letters you make special mention of the fact that, through fifty days, she took no food, I recall that at that time I was at Siena, where she herself also was then, and that she, after she received Communion on Passion Sunday[2] (or, to tell the truth, Palm Sunday, for which of the two Sundays mentioned it was does not fully occur to my memory, but I well recall that it was from then up to the day of the Lord's Ascension exclusive), she took no bodily food, as all asserted, who associated with her night and day. In truth, for some days before the aforesaid feast of the Ascension she was very extenuated in body and made very weak, to such a degree that she was hardly able to speak loud enough to be heard and understood, even putting one's ears next to her mouth, such that we altogether thought that she would die in a short time. At length, on the vigil of the Lord's Ascension, when Vespers had been said in the convent, we went (three pairs of friars, if I recall well) to visit her, fearing that perhaps she would die. However, when the bell was rung for Compline,

---

[2] At this time the Fifth Sunday of Lent was called Passion Sunday.

wishing to return to the convent, I approached her and said to her: "O mother, do you believe that at the present you will leave us?" But she responded to me: "I know not what will be, but I hold it for certain that on this solemnity, either God will show mercy towards me, calling me to Himself as I wish, or, if He does not wish to do this, He shall make me live in a wondrous and unaccustomed manner for the rest of my life." Having heard these things, we all departed.

But at dawn of the following day, she who for so many days beforehand had lain as if dead called her daughter in the Lord, Alessia, in a clear and loud voice, saying to her:"Give me my shoes and mantle." Alessia, marveling and rejoicing, did as she had bid. And Catherine, putting her shoes on her feet, taking her mantle, immediately hurried to the church with such haste that her aforesaid beloved daughter, following her as was customary, was in no way able catch up to her, until Catherine herself had already taken her place in the church to pray. At length, on that morning, in the accustomed way she received Communion with many other fellow-sisters; and afterwards, according to her custom, taken away from her senses, she remained in church with many others of her daughters, until the friars had come to the church, having finished lunch, singing thanks in the accustomed manner. And when the praises were finished, many of us approached her. But she, rising from prayer all cheerful and agreeable, by her most sweet speech gladdened all, women and men, who were there, with a certain ineffable spiritual joy. But afterwards, she added: "Today is a feast of the Lord; I believe that our sweet Savior wishes, for your consolation, that today I should eat with you." Having heard this, all the women who were there went with gladness to eat lunch with her. Therefore, since nothing had been prepared for lunch, we brothers sent them in a pot some of the beans which the convent had cooked for the friars. And thus all the women ate with her that morning, exulting. Therefore there was no small joy among all the different persons who had heard these things, whence many of them came that day out of admiration and joy to visit her, and for their consolation she was compelled that same day to take food and taste wine many times.

However, on the next day she took her place to eat with her daughters, but although she chewed the food, nonetheless she could not swallow it down, nor taste wine. Moreover, when lunch was completed, she began to feel a vehement pain in her stomach, for which reason she was compelled completely to empty her stomach by force, and thus that pain ceased. On the following day also, she ate in the same manner, and, troubled immediately by a pain of the stomach in the manner already mentioned, she was again compelled to empty her stomach forcibly, and the pain ceased. Consequently, she acted in the same way every day, nor would that pain of the stomach cease until she had forcibly brought forth from her stomach the water and all the juices which she had swallowed with a long stalk of fennel.

This report flew here and there and very many were scandalized. For certain ones were suspecting that she did this maliciously, believing that she would do this openly, but would eat in secret, so that evidently she could by this means acquire for herself a reputation of sanctity. Others, moreover, thinking more piously and not believing that she would do this falsely, thought that it was an illusion of the devil, namely so that she might either kill herself by not eating, or else be in danger of vain glory.

Moved by these suspicions, her confessor, Fra Tommaso della Fonte, whose companion I was, himself wondering whether it was an illusion of the devil (for from the testimony of her companions he was certain that she was not feigning), commanded her by obedience that ,after eating food just as has been said, she ought not to bring about vomiting. Moreover, she herself, as a true daughter of obedience, did as had been commanded her. For she observed his commands just as if they were openly sounding to her from Heaven. However, she immediately began to be gravely weakened, such that she almost seemed to be near to death. Having seen this for many hours, her aforesaid confessor, having compassion for her together with many others of us who were present, fearing also lest he should perhaps be the cause of her death, greatly moved by the admonitions of those standing by and also by his own conscience, gave her license to provoke her stomach to vomit. She did so, and immediately she was delivered.

Moreover, when we, marveling, afterwards asked her what and from where this was, she responded that this had been inflicted on her by God in penance for her sin. For she said that she had, in past years, been too voracious in eating herbs and fruits. But afterwards, grieved in heart, she many times had asked God earnestly that he might deign to punish her in the present life for this sin, in which she seemed to have specially offended God. For which reason also, she herself called the aforementioned daily torture of the violent vomiting that has been mentioned "holy justice." Therefore, from that time and thenceforth for many years, that is, for all the remainder of her life, she would every day eat raw herbs, vegetables or legumes cooked with oil, and sometimes cheese (but of the moldy sort, as it is called) -- or, to speak more truly, she would chew these things, drinking pure water. However, rising from the table, she would immediately go to the afore-mentioned torment of purging, often saying with a cheerful countenance: "Let us go to the holy justice." And when this purging was completed, would remain quite free from the said pain of the stomach.

SECOND

Many things also occur to my memory, which I think will be for the edification and consolation of the readers. For when I had already for many years associated with this same holy virgin, she began often to confess her sins sacramentally [to me] and frequently to receive the sacrament of the Eucharist from my hands. Moreover, she would receive this sacrament of the Eucharist with such a great desire of mind and affection of devotion and fervor of spirit that before I could touch the Host to her mouth, while still holding it in my fingers, I would sometimes feel the Host itself be snatched from my fingers by a certain violence, such that I was greatly amazed within me, and in the very beginning, that is, when I began to minister to her the Sacrament of the Eucharist, I sometimes wondered because of this whether the Host had fallen on the ground. However, in the process of time, since I would be more attentive concerning this and would see the Host itself fly off, as it were, into her mouth, and then also since others asserted that this same thing had happened to them, I began, removing all fear and doubt, to venerate it reverently in my mind as something divine, as was due.

When, moreover, after she had taken the Host, we would offer her wine in the chalice to cleanse the mouth, as is customary, she would grip the mouth of the chalice with her teeth with such tenacity that with great difficulty and cleverness we were barely able to extract it from her mouth. Whence also in two silver chalices given to her for the love of God, which she had for the use of her chapel, there were in the tops of them the manifest marks of her most tenacious biting with the teeth, such that it was a marvel that her teeth were not broken.

For when she had received the Host, her mind would be so caught up in God that she would immediately lose the use of the exterior senses, and the members of her body would grow rigid, such that they could more easily be broken than bent, and thus she would remain every day for about three hours and more, completely absorbed and insensible. Often, also, when she was placed in such ecstasy, speaking with God, she would utter deep and devout prayers and petitions. Hearing these words, those who were present, as commonly happened, would be moved to pious and devout tears. These prayers were for the most part redacted in writing word for word: some indeed by me, but many through others, when she, as has been said, was uttering them with a clear and distinct voice. For the sake of brevity, I refrain from going on about their profundity. For these words and the sense of the words do not at all appear to be those of a woman, but the doctrine and opinions of a great doctor. And truly thus it was because it was not she herself, but the Spirit, who was speaking through her, as is clearly apparent to every pious reader of those prayers.

THIRD

Moreover, her confessions in those days were not about some sin committed or perpetrated, but only about the omission of perfect virtue and ingratitude for the benefits of God, whence she would call herself wretched and miserable. For these were her words, and she would even say affirmatively that she was more miserable than all men and that she was the cause of all the evils that were happening. I, however, where I ought to have been edified and have profited, began in my mind, from my ignorance and slothfulness, to interpret badly her words, so holy and so profound, like an animal man who does not perceive the things which are of God. For I was thinking that in her mind she did not believe herself to be such as she repeatedly said with her voice that she was.

Therefore, moved by such a bestial suspicion, after I had many times heard such and similar words, I questioned her, intending somewhat to prove her wrong: "How," I said, "do you say this, since it is manifest to all that you abhor the sins which many perpetrate with delight every day?" And she, sighing, responded to me: "O father, as I see, you all do not know my misery. For I, wretched one, have received gifts from my Creator so many and so great and of such a kind, that, as I think, there is not any ribald so vile that if he had received such things, he would not burn entirely, inflamed with love for his Creator. And thus, both by example of life and by the word of teaching, he would enkindle the hearts of men to love of the heavenly fatherland and contempt of the present life, and thus men would cease from their sins. Therefore, since I, wretched one, endowed with so many gifts, do not do this, what can I say about myself, acknowledging the truth, except that I am most ungrateful to my God and that I am the cause of the ruin of all those who through me could have been called back from evil and advanced to the good, if I, as I ought to, had called them back with the food of God's word and animated them to act well by the example of a good life? And since I have not done these things as I ought, without doubt I am guilty." I, having heard these things, blushed and was silent, and rightly so. For while, as I already said, I was thinking that she was worthy of blame, she, by humbly accusing herself, showed me to be guilty in many ways.

FOURTH

Moreover, just as I recall having said in my aforesaid attestations, so much grace was poured out in the heart and on the lips of the holy virgin that she would not only know the disposition of soul of those coming to her, but also with her fiery utterances she would so inflame their hearts that, as commonly happened, they would change their life for the better. And although many such things have been described in the *Legenda*, and also in my affirmations I have made mention of certain such things, nevertheless because certain things, worthy of narration and specially known to me, still occur to my memory, therefore I will here recite one of the many, omitting all the others for the sake of brevity.

For while she was still dwelling in the seclusion of her cell, that is, before she had come forth by the command of God into the public through association with others (for at that time, except for her father and her brothers, she would not speak to any man, except by the special permission of her confessor), nonetheless the odor of her sanctity and reputation began to be diffused through the whole city of Siena.

But, just as the Apostle, writing to the Corinthians (2 Corinthians 2:16), said about himself and those like him that as the good odor of Christ they were for some an odor of life leading to life, but for others an odor of death leading to death (that is, as the *Gloss* explains in the same place, the life and doctrine of the apostles was for the good and faithful an odor of life leading to life, but for the unfaithful and hostile an odor of death leading to death), so also it happened concerning this holy virgin. For the simple and humble of heart venerated her and commended her and praised her works; but certain men and women, that is the false-hearted and the hostile, mocked her and spoke ill of her, thinking that if she said anything rightly and prudently, she was drawing it all from us

86

friars, and believing that we were instructing her to speak thus so as to acquire the vain-glory and pomp of the world.

Now among her other distinguished persecutors in this region there was a certain Fra Lazarino of Pisa, of the Order of Minors, who at that time was lecturing in philosophy in the convent of his order in Siena with great renown. For he was outstanding in intellect and was very fluent in speech, and also popular among the people in his sermons. He, hearing that a reputation of good odor was spread through the city concerning the holy virgin, and driven by the goad of envy, strove to detract from the reputation of the virgin, not only in secret among his own, but even in public among strangers. Moreover, his zeal against the holy virgin blazed up and raged so much that he hated not only her, but also all those whom he knew to be of her household. For this reason, since he knew that I was of the household of the same holy virgin, he also intensely hated me (I was at that time lecturing on the *Sentences* in the same place in my turn), so much that he strove with all his might to render me hateful to all the students, especially when we would all convene together for a disputation, as is the custom.

However, when, through the teaching of experience, he realized that he was making no headway by such detraction, but that every day the great reputation of her sanctity was increasing, he decided to denigrate her reputation in his public sermons to the people with all his efforts. And when he did not seem to be succeeding this way either, he made plans to visit her cunningly under the appearance of devotion, that thus he might catch her in her words or deeds as worthy of calumny.

Therefore, on the vigil of Blessed Catherine [of Alexandria, virgin and martyr][3], he came at the evening hour to my cell, asking me to bring him to speak with her. Now I, believing that he was asking this with compunction of heart, consented; and came to her by license of the virgin's own confessor, that is, Fra Tomasso della Fonte. Therefore, entering her cell, Fra Lazarino sat upon some small box; she, however, sat near his feet on the pavement, while I sat apart on the opposite side. He was silent for some time, and she was silent. At length, he said, rising: "1 came to you willingly having heard such a good report of your holiness, and that you are gifted by the Lord in understanding of the Scriptures, hoping to hear something both edifying and consoling to my

---

[3] November 24

87

soul." But she responded: "I rejoiced in your arrival, believing that the Lord had sent you so that you, who have a knowledge of the holy scriptures by which you feed every day the souls of the peoples, might come moved by charity to console my poor little soul; and thus, for the love of Jesus Christ, I ask that you deign to do."

When, therefore, the time was slipping by in this manner of speaking, and already night was approaching, he, not mocking her, as he had thought he would do, but nonetheless not appreciating her much in his heart, but rather thinking little of her, said: "I see that the hour is late, and therefore I think that it is better that I go, and some other time I will be able to return at a more fitting hour," and thus he rose to go. And while he was going away, the holy virgin followed him; moreover, kneeling and with arms crossed, she asked him to bless her: which he also did. Having received this blessing, she asked that in his prayers he should recommend her. But he, moved more by a certain embarrassment than by devotion, asked her to pray for him: and she promised that she would willingly do this. Therefore, he went away, as has been said, thinking little of her, believing that she was indeed good, but not worthy of such a great reputation as was flying about concerning her.

When, therefore, on the following night, he was rising immediately to meditate upon the lesson, which according to the custom he would have to read to his disciples in the morning, tears suddenly began to flow from his eyes in great abundance, tears which, the more he wiped them, the more they multiplied and abounded. He marveled and labored long in wiping the tears which were flowing continuously and abundantly, and he sought within himself the cause of so much weeping, nor could he find it; he wavered in spirit, seeking the cause, whether this happened from too much drinking in the evening or perhaps because he slept with his head not covered: he found neither of these to be the cause of this sort of weeping.

Meanwhile the time was slipping away, and the accustomed hour of lecturing was at hand. The disciples were soliciting the teacher to enter the classroom. He indeed, forcing himself as far as he was able, came quickly to the classroom, but, lecturing in a perfunctory manner, he suddenly stopped because he could not contain his tears. And so, returning to his cell, soon relaxing the reins of his tears, he groaned with a great cry, and, angry at himself, he began to reproach himself, saying to himself: "What do you have, Lazarino? What do you want? Has your mother suddenly died? Or has your brother been slain by the sword?"

Occupying that day with these and similar words, hardly tasting food or drink, he arrived to the silence of the night, which was welcome to him. And when the time came, he fell asleep for a little while, overcome by weariness and sorrow; and rising again, and once again, as before, not being able to contain his tears, he began to think that perhaps in some grave matter, unknown to him, he was offending God, on account of which God was thus mercifully calling him back to Himself. Therefore, while he was attentively meditating about this, a voice sounded loudly in the ears not of his body but of his mind, saying to him: "Or perhaps has it so quickly slipped from your memory that yesterday you despised my faithful servant Catherine with such a proud mind, and that, although insincerely, you nonetheless commended yourself to her prayers?"

Having heard this inner voice, gladdened in mind he wanted to weep for joy, but he could not in any way: for immediately that flow of tears was so dried up that he could not put forth even one tear. Nonetheless, immediately his heart was inflamed and burned with the desire of visiting the holy virgin herself. For which reason, his mind was afflicted, as it were, by a certain sadness and weariness, since the dawn was not beginning to shine as quickly as he wished from the ardor of his desire to see her. Therefore, not waiting for the rising of the sun, but in the twilight of the day, going out of his convent he hastened very quickly and unashamed to the virgin's house. And when he knocked at the door of her cell, the holy virgin, not ignorant of the things which were being done by her Spouse in that man, opened the door.

But he, as soon as he saw her, before he entered the cell, prostrated himself at the virgin's feet. Yet the virgin, not enduring this, cast herself to the ground similarly, asking him to rise. And since he refused to do this, at length they both rose from the earth together. Moreover, entering the cell, he in no way wished to sit in a high place as he had done before, but on the terrace which was covered by a mat of rushes; the virgin, moreover, remained seated similarly on the ground. And when he had had a long and holy colloquy with her, completely serene in mind he offered himself entirely to the same holy virgin, asking her earnestly that she deign to accept him as her son and to direct and educate him as a son in the way of God.

But when she said that he knew the way of God better, by means of the Sacred Scriptures, he responded that he knew it in the outer rind, but she tasted it in the inner part. At length, overcome by his insistent prayers, she responded: "The way of salvation for your soul is that, spurning the pomp of the age and all the complacency of the world, and casting away money and all superfluous things, you should, naked and humble, follow Christ crucified and your holy father, Blessed Francis." He, hearing this, seeing that the vanity of his heart lay open to the virgin, confused in mind and truly unsettled in heart, immediately was changed into another man: indeed, breaking forth into tears, he immediately promised that he would do each and every thing which she had commanded him to do.

And the outcome of the matter also proved this. For within a few days he distributed everything, the money which he had, his extra clothes, and even his books, except a certain commentary on the Gospels necessary for preaching, and he became in reality a true poor man of Christ. Therefore, having been made Paul from Saul, that is, a humble man from a proud, he was also made from a persecutor into a preacher. For just as, before, both before his brothers and before outsiders, he used to always detract from the reputation of the holy virgin, and both in private and also in public, as has been said, he used to eagerly denigrate her reputation, so henceforth he began, accusing himself, to extol and marvelously commend her.

For this reason, just like Saul who had been made Paul, he suffered many and grave persecutions, especially from his own. For they said that he had become insane, both because he was publicly extolling her whose reputation he was accustomed a little while before to uproot with all his efforts, and because, as has been said, he had abdicated from himself all temporal things except only the things necessary, and they believed that he was too pompous, and that later he would regret having done this. But he, comforted frequently by her, recovered his strength like another Paul and overcame all of them. Indeed, as I said, he suffered many and grave persecutions, which to narrate would be too lengthy. Nevertheless, with God's help, and by the merits of that spouse of Christ, he triumphed over them all. Moreover he lived many years after this, very laudably progressing daily from good to better. Indeed, he gained many souls for Christ, both by the word of preaching with which he was especially endowed, and also by the example of his good works in which, as has been said, he progressed daily and persevered even unto the end of life.

Each and every one of the aforesaid things in this chapter, although narrated by me in a diminished and incomplete way, I myself know partly from the teaching of experience, and partly from the narration of it to me by the friar himself, who was later truly a family member to me.

After this, with the fame of the virgin's sanctity growing daily, many began to come together to her, men as well as women, with the aforesaid venerable father urging all to this, in private speeches as well as also in public preaching to the people. Also, many notable citizens were at that time wondrously transformed by her into a better life, of some of whom special mention has been made in the ordinary *Legenda* and similarly in my above-written attestations.

Also, many religious of diverse orders would come to her, and, one and all, well consoled and excellently edified by her, going away they would implore her with prayers that they be able to come to her and visit her again; not only the younger and ignorant ones but also the elders and many of the learned were marvelously changed by her for the better, just as is manifestly clear of Master Gabriele da Volterra, of the Order of Friars Minor, who was a man very famous through all of Italy in the knowledge and skill of preaching; and nonetheless, having heard her, he was, out of admiration, changed in spirit, and would often visit her devoutly.

This same thing is also evident concerning Fra Giovanni Terzo, a good and aged Master of Sacred Theology of the Order of Hermits of St. Augustine from Siena, and also concerning Fra Felice di Massa, a good Lecturer in the aforesaid order: both of these associated for many years with her in Siena, and afterwards, at the time of Pope Gregrory XI of happy memory, they remained in Avignon with her for four months, and also returned to Italy with her. Also, this aforesaid Master Giovanni accompanied her afterwards when she went to Rome at the time of Pope Urban VI of happy memory, and dwelt with her there daily up to the day of the happy passing of the holy virgin from this world to her Spouse.

Why should I delay more, desiring to enumerate how many and which prelates of diverse churches and also abbots, notable men of diverse orders, would come together to her and venerate her with special affection, as is more amply clear about some of them in the *Legenda*?—and thus here I pass on from these.

When, afterwards, we were at Pisa and no small multitude of either sex was coming together to her in order to hear her, some of them, genuflecting out of devotion, were kissing her hand. But certain men, gravely scandalized by this, were murmuring against her, trying with all their might to turn away all those they could from the devotion which they showed themselves to have towards her.

Moreover, among the others was one outstanding man, well experienced in the art of medicine, named Master Giovanni Gittalebracia. This man, bearing quite impatiently the fact that he was not able to hold back, as he wished, the people coming to her, thought to confuse her by proposing to her grave questions of Sacred Scripture. For it had sounded abroad that she was explaining the Sacred Scripture. Moreover, that more credence might be given to his detraction, which he was intending to make against her, he brought with him by his persuasions a certain expert in the law who was called Signor Pietro Albizi, who was of advanced age, and both in knowledge and manners was a man of great gravity.

Therefore, both of them, coming to her, sat down alone with her. And the aforesaid Master Giovanni, who was younger, beginning to speak, said to her: "Signor Pietro, who is here, and I, hearing your good reputation, and that you are learned in the Sacred Scriptures, have come desiring to hear something from your mouth for our consolation. Moreover, I wish especially to hear from you how it is understood that Scripture says that God, creating the world, 'spoke and they were made.'" And he added: "Surely God does not have a mouth and tongue?" And examining her on many other things, at length he was silent, seeking an answer concerning the things proposed by him.

But she, opening her mouth, said: "I wonder greatly that you, who are teachers of others, should say that you come to hear one little woman, since it would be more appropriate that you should teach me, as the ignorant one. But nonetheless, since it pleases you that I should respond, I will speak as the Lord shall grant. What does it pertain to me, or what use does it bring to me to know how God, who is not a body but only spirit, created the world by speaking? But I see that it is useful, nay necessary, for me and also for you to know this, namely, that the Lord Jesus Christ, true son of God, took our nature for our salvation, suffered and died for our liberation; to know this is necessary to me for salvation, that believing and meditating on these things my heart might be enkindled to love of Him who has loved me thus."

As she was saying these and similar things with great fervor of spirit, the aforesaid Signor Pietro, deeply moved in his heart, could not contain his tears; and so, rising, with head uncovered, kneeling he asked pardon from her. But she, not enduring this, prostrated herself to the earth, earnestly asking him to rise. Since he refused, after a long and pious struggle about this, both of them, rising at the same time from the earth, sat down together. Moreover, afterwards, when they had had a long and sweet colloquy between them about the things pertaining to the soul's salvation, at length the same Signor Pietro, again removing his hood, beseeched the same virgin that she would deign to hold at baptism the child which he hoped shortly to have from his wife: which she both kindly promised and afterwards carried out in deed. Also, the aforesaid Master Giovanni, pierced to the heart, having humbly sought pardon from her and received no small consolation, went away together with the same Signor Pietro, completely changed in spirit and well edified by her, and thenceforth he changed his detractions into praise and commendation of the virgin.

Fifth

At about the same time, Fra Raimondo, her confessor, who afterwards composed her *Legenda*, moved by the ferocity of murmurings, questioned her alone, with only myself present, saying: "O mother, do you not see how many reverences are being shown to you by those who come to you? And since you do not prohibit them, it seems to many that you take delight in these things; and thus many are scandalized and murmur against you." And he added: "Is it possible, mother, that so many honors and reverences, which are made to you by so many, would not move your mind to some empty glory?"

She, responding to the things asked, said to the first: "Indeed, as very often I do not notice such reverences, neither, by God's grace, do they please me; but when they come offered to me, I consider the good affection of those coming and I give thanks to the Divine Goodness that moves them thus, and in my mind I ask that He who moves them might also perfect and fulfill the desires which He Himself has inspired."

Moreover, to the second she responded thus: "I marvel that a creature, knowing itself to be a creature, could have vainglory." We, marveling at such a response, were silent. I confess that at that time I did not understand this saying. But in the process of time, in ruminating and meditating on the aforementioned saying, it seemed to me, and even now it seems, that she did not wish to say anything except to agree with the teaching of the Apostle (1 Corinthians 4), which says in this regard: "What do you have that you have not received?" And immediately he adds: "But if you have received it, why do you glory as if you have not received it?" Nor do I say this because I believe that she had read this in the epistles of the Apostle Paul and thus, as if appealing to him, she responded to us. For I do not believe this, but I believe and firmly hold that the same One who taught the apostle Paul and made him a vessel of election, that is, a treasury of the Sacred Scriptures, Himself taught this, His beloved spouse, and not only this thing which has been mentioned above, but He also delivered to her many other useful and very noteworthy teachings, while He so familiarly deigned to converse with her, as in her *Legenda* it can be seen at greater length, and is more openly contained. I myself also inserted something about this matter, although briefly and crudely, in my attestations.

Moreover, that it might more manifestly appear that the above-written response of the holy virgin emanated from the doctrine which she had long before, as has been said, received from our Savior, let us bring back to our memory, if it is not tiresome, the first teaching which the holy virgin herself confessed that she had from the Lord in the beginning of her familiar conversation with Him. For the Savior would say to her: "Daughter, I want you to learn who I am and who you are. For I am Who am. But you are she who is not. If you know well these two things, you will be blessed, for you will always be humble and obedient to my commands, knowing that I am the Creator and Lord, but that you are the creature and the useless servant of your Lord. By this doctrine, you will evade all the snares of the enemy, whose exercise and effort is always to urge on the minds of the incautious their own reputation and self-love, even to the contempt of me. But by this doctrine you will know that you are nothing of yourself. But if you are anything, this you have from me, and thus you ought always to despise yourself and always to magnify me." Concerning this original teaching given by our Savior to the holy virgin, as for the foundation of the spiritual edifice, there is a treatment at the beginning of the tenth chapter of the first part of the *Legenda* of the holy virgin, where it is also explained more broadly and clearly.

Sixth

Also in those days, while the virgin was staying in Pisa, a certain man of no small reputation, known among spiritual persons as Il Bianco di Città di Castello, hearing about such a universal coming together of all people to the holy virgin, and about the honor and reverences which were commonly exhibited to her by all, inflamed and moved by zeal, addressed to the same holy virgin a certain letter, lengthy and well-dictated, in which he sharply reprehended her, because she allowed such things to be done concerning her.

For he alleged to the contrary the deeds and teachings of the Savior, and also the doctrine and examples of the saints, adding also that such a manner of living seemed to be dangerous and more to be vituperated than commended. He also exhorted her to flee the public and seek solitude, concluding that this is the life of the saints, but that the other is the life of hypocrites and those who seek their own praise.

This letter arrived first to the hands of Fra Raimondo, the confessor already mentioned. And having read it through, both he and I (who was present)—greatly moved by anger against the writer, thinking that he wrote thus not out of charity, but out of jealousy and stirred by the goad of envy—conferred together, saying that it would be good not to present the said letter to the holy virgin herself, but to write back against him and harshly rebuke him as someone rash and ignorant of the spiritual life.

While we were thus muttering for a long time, and sometimes raising the voice higher between us, the holy virgin, who was not far removed from us, took note that we were thus deeply stirred. Therefore, she made us be called to her there. But having heard the cause of our disturbance, she said: "Give me the letter that I may read it." However, Fra Raimondo did not wish to deliver it to her, intending to do what we had said at first. But she said: "Even if you do not wish to give it to me, at least, since it is directed to me, I ought to hear it." Therefore, Fra Raimondo read the letter, while the holy virgin herself listened.

And while, in her presence, we were both raging together against the writer of that letter, she, kindly rebuking us, said: "You ought to give thanks together with me to the one who sent this letter, since you see that he so sweetly and openly admonishes concerning my salvation. And he also, fearing lest I be deceived in the way of God, so prudently renders me cautious against the wiles of my enemy. Hence, you and I are obliged to his charity. Therefore, I wish to have this letter and to respond and thank him"; which she also did, laudably and most virtuously, as is clearly apparent to one who reads that letter. Moreover, when Fra Raimondo still insisted that he also wanted to respond and rebuke him, she forbade it altogether, with a stern countenance, rebuking us for such great impatience, and because we interpreted a good work as evil.

Therefore, thus equally by word and example she restrained us daily from vices and sweetly encouraged us to acts and works of the virtues, although I (to speak not without shame and embarrassment at myself), like the arid land, brought forth almost no fruit of good work from such an affluent and open heavenly doctrine, which the display of her works confirmed.

Nonetheless, in many other persons of either sex it did not result thus. For of them, many, like good land, produced most abundant fruits of good works, people whose names I will omit to insert here for the sake of brevity, and also because there is special mention made of many such persons in the *Legenda*.

Therefore, the foregoing are the things which occur to me at present as needing to be supplied after the things narrated by me in my above-mentioned attestations. And let these things suffice as far as the first heading is concerned.

II

Against the second defect: Concerning the explanation and declaration by the witness of certain things said in his above-named attestations, which seemed not to conform to the things said in the *Legenda* of the virgin. This declaration is corresponding to three things said in the attestations mentioned,

- of which the first was concerning the virgin's disgrace, and the retraction of the same, made by a certain fellow-sister Andrea the washing of whose wound the virgin swallowed; this seemed to be told otherwise in the *Legenda*;
- the second was concerning the motive of the first passing of the virgin about which it seemed that it was held otherwise in the *Legenda*;

- the third, moreover, was concerning the pains of the stigmata which remained in the body of the virgin up to the end of her life, since nonetheless the opposite seems to be contained in the *Legenda*;
- and also concerning a fourth declaration of an error of events related in the wrong order:

Lady Andrea

And so, we proceed to the second heading, namely where you say that certain things which I narrate in my aforesaid attestations seem to contradict the narration of the *Legenda* about the same matters, especially about the restitution of reputation made by the lady Andrea, which I wrote was made after the drinking of that most foul pus, but in the *Legenda*, as you say, it is contained that the cause of the retraction of the said infamy was a certain vision shown to the said Andrea.

To this I respond first that my aforesaid narration does not contradict the *Legenda*, although I do not make mention of that vision. For often in the Gospels you find that one Evangelist narrates the same story in full, but another narrates the same one in a truncated way. I omit to insert here examples of this matter for the sake of brevity, and also because they are known to those accustomed to read the Gospels. Nonetheless, they are not said for that reason to contradict each other, as Augustine clearly teaches in the book *On the Concordance of the Evangelists.*

Secondly, I respond that I recall that I heard about that vision in those times, but when I wrote the attestations mentioned above, at that time it did not occur to my memory, nor is that a wonder, since forty and perhaps more years have passed since I heard it; indeed, forgetfulness is naturally concomitant upon old age. Therefore, although I did not insert that vision in my narration, nonetheless I did not deny it, which would be to contradict the *Legenda*; nor do I deny it, but I confirm it.

Similarly, if the *Legenda* narrates that that disgrace came at the time of the sickness of the said lady Andrea, but I in my narration maintain that that disgrace preceded the time of the sickness of the same Andrea, I think that I have written the truth since there was another occasion of that disgrace than that which is put in the *Legenda*, which I omitted and omit to narrate, because the narration would be too long and the usefulness nothing. Nor on this account do I contradict the *Legenda*, since it is possible that just as before her sickness she defamed the holy virgin as I narrate, so also at the time of her sickness she did the same thing again, as the *Legenda* narrates.

First Passing[4]

Moreover, to that which you say concerning the motive of the first passing of the holy virgin out of this light, I find no conflict of the things I said with the narration of the *Legenda*. For in the *Legenda* it is said that her heart broke from the violence of divine love, and was split from the top downwards, and from this she died. However, I in my attestations say the same thing, but I do not tell it in the same manner nor so completely as in the *Legenda*. Nonetheless, no contradiction follows from this.

Stigmata

But with the third point, you say that my narration about the stigmata seems to contradict the narration of the *Legenda*, because I say there that the said pains, together with the pains of the other sufferings of the holy virgin, namely of her head, chest, and hips, continued in her up to the end of her life; the *Legenda* however narrates that, at the insistence of her sons and daughters in Christ, she asked the Lord that, if it would be for the better, He might remove from her those pains of the stigmata, which were so dire that they would necessarily have violently wrenched away her bodily life within a few days, and the *Legenda* adds that she was heard and that the wounds did not afflict her body but rather comforted it.

Here, I say that I believe that what the *Legenda* says is true, and I affirm that it was thus because I was present there, when all those things were done just as the *Legenda* narrates. Nonetheless, it was possible, saving the aforesaid truth of the *Legenda*, that those pains, so dire and bitter, were so mitigated by the Lord through her prayers that for that reason they were said not to afflict the body, but rather to comfort it, just as the tepid, in comparison with the exceedingly warm, appears cold, although it is not. And so thus, because they were more mild, the pains seemed to her not dire and bitter, but sweet and consoling, just as

---

[4] Catherine's "first passing" is a reference to her "mystical death" described in Raymond of Capua's *Legenda*, Part Two, Chapter VI (no. 213, pp. 201+, in Conleth Kearns' English translation).

happened to her concerning the pains of her other sufferings already mentioned.

For as in my attestations I said in the chapter which begins, "Therefore, the holy virgin, considering, etc.", she, for a certain refreshment of her spirit against the tedium which proceeded from the prolongation of her stay in this present life, asked of the Lord that he grant her as a gift the sufferings already mentioned; and when he had commanded these and she was gravely afflicted, she was not sad nor disturbed, but merry and joyful, as follows in the same place.

The *Legenda* also, in the same sixth chapter of the second part, cited a little while before now, asserts this same thing, namely that she asked of the Lord that all the aforesaid sufferings be given to her as a singular gift. And thus it is manifestly apparent that those pains did not afflict her, but rather they were a singular refreshment to her, since through those pains, asked from the Lord, she saw herself in some way conformed to her most exceedingly loving Spouse, Christ, in His pains. And so thus they also did not afflict her body intolerably, that is to say as before, but rather they comforted her, namely from the abundance of spiritual joy which they generated in her mind. And so thus, as I wrote, perhaps those pains remained in her body up to the end of her life, although mitigated in this manner.

And lest this interpretation of mine should seem too extreme, you will find a similar manner of speaking in the already-cited sixth chapter of the second part of the *Legenda*; where beyond the middle of the said chapter it literally reads thus: "As a proof or indication of this, she said that the rest of the pains in her body had passed, and that that one alone had remained." And immediately it goes on: "Whence, although she continually suffered pains of the hip and pains of the head without ceasing, nonetheless, she said that this pain was more vehement, etc."

One could also perhaps respond not inappropriately and in a different manner: namely, that not each and every word of this or any other *Legenda* should be so weighed and pondered as if they were words of the Sacraments or the Gospels, to which it is not permitted to anyone to add or change one iota or part of a letter.

Moreover, I notice that I have written certain things in an order contrary to that of the *Legenda* here and also in my often-mentioned attestations: which error is to be tolerated, as long as the truth of the fact remains, for the Evangelists too sometimes narrate thus the deeds of the Lord Savior, as is clear through Blessed Augustine in his book, already cited. Therefore, you or anyone else ought not to be scandalized, nor yet to marvel if the *Legenda* and I or anyone else narrate something variously, as long as there is not truly a contradiction in the narration. And let these things suffice as far as the second heading is concerned.

6

The Spiritual Life in the Teaching of St. Catherine of Siena

Antoine Lemonnyer, O.P.

First Part[1]

I. The Spiritual Life

At the beginning of these studies, or rather of these informal talks on the mystical doctrine of St. Catherine of Siena, may I be permitted, by way of introduction, to make a confidential observation? I hasten to add that it is to my own embarrassment, which encourages me to make it.

There was a time when my relish for the writings of this dear saint was very mediocre indeed. I had for them only that impersonal appreciation which remains on the surface of the soul and is almost a mere lip-service. I found them too intellectual, too abstract, too dogmatic or else not dogmatic enough. Nourished, like all the brethren, upon the lofty teaching of St. Thomas, accustomed to the safe procedures of theological exposition, to the explicitly proven affirmations, the search for the final causes of divine things insofar as they are accessible to us, I was disconcerted and disappointed by what is less consequential and systematic, less logical and more intuitive in St. Catherine's style. I did not find her rational enough, dogmatic enough for my taste.

Or else, on the contrary, she was too much so. When I felt the need of refreshing my soul with the living waters of mystical teachings and occurrences, it was not to her that I went most spontaneously. The great German mystics, Meister Eckhart, Tauler, Henry Suso attracted me more.

---

[1] For the Forward in the original edition, see Appendix A, p. 177. For the Table of Contents in the original edition, see Appendix B, p. 181.

Their ambiguous language, which Bossuet judged with severity, is full of suggestion and savor. Their thought is clothed in the magnificent apparel of Rhenish poetry; and amid this symbolic setting, behind the tenuous veil of their terminology the divine realities appear like approaching shadows. While reading them the mind, long held at tension over the powerful but austere text of St. Thomas, became delightfully relaxed while the heart expanded. Even the more imaginative, bizarre, lower forms, so to speak, of mystical doctrine and experience,--those which Huysmans prefers and describes so accurately and vividly, although somewhat heavily at times—appealed to my soul occasionally. This was a different aspect of divine things unrevealed by rational theology. But above all, I had recourse with all my soul to the writings of the Church Fathers, those works blossoming in the springtide of Christianity and abounding in spiritual sap, like the buds in April. The Fathers of the Church are primitives, the Angelicos, Van den Weydens, and Memlings of spiritual doctrine. It is among them, in a Clement of Alexandria, a St. Augustine, a St. Ambrose, that one discovers, in all its purity, the Christian spirit.

One thing, nevertheless, will always impel even those who have not yet broken the seals that enclose St. Catherine's doctrine to keep in touch with her writings: the admirable language she uses. It is impossible not to be attracted by that old Tuscan speech, its enchanting richness of sound, its long, flowing, vibrant sentences, developing each elegant phrase with so much assurance, ease, grace and evident delight, under the splendid light of a thought ever lucid and clear. Enraptured by the grave, gentle charm emanating from them, one continues to read. Gradually one becomes interested in the subject matter itself and begins to appreciate its value. At last, one surrenders to the dictum of the best judges who place St. Catherine in the first rank among the doctors of mysticism. She is an incomparable mistress of the interior life, a soul rich, perhaps beyond any other, in supernatural lights and experiences. Hers is a mind as solid and well-balanced as it is lofty and penetrating. She is a psychologist of the highest school with an admirable knowledge of the human soul to its very depths. Added to this, she possesses all the distinguished grace of an Italian already bordering on the brilliant period of the *quattrocento.* Her conception of the spiritual life is as far from esoteric, as universal, as can be. She approaches the absolute.

The author of these modest studies would wish to try to share these convictions with those of his readers who do not yet agree with them. At least, he would like to facilitate for them the personal, direct contact with St. Catherine of Siean's writings, hoping that they may be increasingly inspired by her doctrine in the conduct of their souls. Today we shall ask St. Catherine of Siena for her conception of the spiritual life, the relationship she perceives between its various elements, what general plan she considers advisable to follow in the supernatural cultivation of oneself. It will be a kind of synthetic previous of her ideas. Nor do I find it necessary to compose this synthesis myself. I discover it all prepared on one of the most powerful pages—despite its frail appearance—that the saint ever wrote, which it will suffice to translate and discuss. Our dear saint will therefore speak in person. Is that not the best and safest way?

⇧

This page of synthesis is to be found in the *Dialogue.* The book was written by St. Catherine, as we know, at the very end of her life and at the express request of her disciples. For them and for her it was her spiritual testament. We find her thought there, consequently, in its definitive form, at the high point of its maturity and perfection. Let us listen with reverence, for it is God Himself who speaks:

> Do you know how these three virtues [humility, discretion, and love] stand together? It is, as if a circle so sweetly planted, produces fragrant blossoms of virtue, with many scents of great variety, inasmuch as the soul renders fruits of grace and of utility to her neighbor, according to the zeal of those who come to receive fruit from My servants; and to Me she renders the sweet odor of glory and praise to My name, and so fulfills the object of her creation. In this way, therefore, she reaches the term of her being, that is Myself, her God, who am Eternal Life. And these fruits cannot be taken from her without her will, inasmuch as they are all flavored with discretion, because they are all united, as has been said before.[2]

---

[2] *Dialogue*, chapter 10. [Translator's note: Whenever possible, the *Dialogue* quotations will be drawn from Algar Thorold's English version (Newman Bookshop, Westerminister, Maryland: 1943); this translation does not have chapter divisions.]

This celebrated allegory, so distinctive in its simplicity, does not perhaps possess in detail all the precision nor even all the coherence one might wish for, such as a professional litterateur would not have failed to produce. One suspects that the saint dictated it to one of her disciples, doubtless in the course of an ecstasy, and that she neglected to revise or improve upon it later. Its meaning is nevertheless quite clear. What interests us for the present in this description is not the various elements of the spiritual life enumerated there, that is, not these elements considered in themselves, but the living unit which they form, the order in which they are joined together. That, moreover, is what God intends to teach His eager pupil. "Do you know," He says, "how these three virtues [humility, discretion, and love] stand together?" We are therefore justified in seeking from this allegory a real plan of the spiritual life, a complete program of interior development, and we shall in fact discover it here.

The tree to be cultivated in our soul, or more exactly divine charity, the love of God which is therein the very principle of the spiritual life. To plant, nourish and cause the love of God to grow within us is—let it not be forgotten—the true object of our interior labors. It is by the progress we make in the love of God that the success of our efforts to tend to perfection can be measured. Nor is this a personal opinion on St. Catherine's part. It is the common teaching of the theologians and masters of the mystical life. It may even be said that this is the teaching of the Church herself and of the Gospel.

To plant and nourish divine charity? But where and how? It requires a suitable soil, a *humus* that will feed it. In what does this soil or *humus* consist according to the thought of St. Catherine? In humility. "Then the tree of love feeds itself on humility," she expressly declares in the page we have just quoted. A little earlier she had said, making use of another figure: "Humility is the foster-mother and nurse of charity."[3] He who would therefore cultivate this divine charity whereby the soul lives supernaturally must heap up in abundance about it, as the base of a rare plant which is being cultivated with tender care, the fertile soul of Christian humility.

But how is this humility itself to be acquired? Whence shall we ask for it? Here the saint shows herself truly a superb psychologist; her reply is

---

[3] *Dialogue*, chapter 9.

worthy of all our attention. Will it be from external practices? From more or less violent efforts of the will? No; it is derived from knowledge, a deliberate conviction of the mind. What knowledge? From the knowledge of self and of God, of self in God, from an accurate view of what we are in relation to God and of what God is in relation to us. "The earth of true humility," she says in her symbolical language, "is as wide as the diameter of the circle." This circle, let us recall, is the knowledge of self in God. Is that not equivalent to saying that true humility is born of self-knowledge, that it is the precise measure of this knowledge? It is not difficult to appreciate that this must necessarily be so. By knowing ourselves better and knowing God more truly, we shall come to judge ourselves at our proper value. We shall penetrate more deeply and accept more readily that great truth so frequently repeated by the eternal Father to St. Catherine which is the very formula of humility: "I am He who is; you art she who is not." An accurate knowledge of what we are in relation to God is therefore, according to our saint, the basis of the whole interior life, the starting point for all spiritual progress. It is the acquisition that we must first apply ourselves. Humility springs spontaneously, as it were, from this interior conviction and thus the tree of charity finds in the Christian soul the fertile soil its nature demands.

Thus favorably planted, the tree of divine love feels like coursing through it, like the sturdy, deep-rooted oak wherein the sap rises in springtime. First of all it puts forth a vigorous branch which is the virtue of discernment or supernatural discretion. This virtue is closely united to the knowledge of self and of God. St. Catherine even goes so far, in the preceding chapter, as to identify them. Supernatural discernment is the knowledge of ourselves in God, animated by charity and becoming the rule of all our conduct. Indeed, what light is not cast upon our pathway by the understanding of what we are and ought to be before God! Spiritual discernment is, basically, the mystical term for Christian prudence; or if you will, it is the highest degree, the most refined form of that virtue. As St. Catherine observes in several places, the supernatural virtue of discretion is absolutely necessary for the conduct of the Christian life. None of us can dispense with it without exposing himself to the gravest mistakes. It is not to be wondered at, then, if this is the first thing our saint expects the tree of charity to produce, the first virtue she urges the Christian virtue to acquire and cultivate, once the foundations of the spiritual life have been laid.

But the sap of the divine tree is not exhausted by this first effort. Now it must blossom forth with a variety of flowers which are the different moral virtues. In fact, it is the practice of the supernatural moral virtues that the Christian who has reached this point in his interior development must henceforth apply himself energetically. Without these virtues there can be no authentic Christian life. Neither a multiplicity of prayers nor of exterior practices of devotion can pretend to take the place of the exercise of the evangelical virtues. On the other hand, it is in the love of God which is charity that the Christian must seek the determining motivation for cultivating them; only thence will he draw the courage necessary for this difficult undertaking. "Virtue is only acquired through love of Me," God declared to St. Catherine. She is therefore justified in representing these virtues as the flowers of charity and in considering this blossoming the first and indispensable proof of the vitality of this divine tree in our souls.

After the flowers come the fruits. Since the tree of charity is covered with blossoms, it must also bear fruits which, according to St. Catherine, are the good of one's neighbor and the honor of God. These, in her system of thought, are in fact the two great incentives to the Christian life, the two passions which inspire it, giving it an impetus and support. She cannot conceive of a Christian soul in whom love of God does not produce this twofold, irresistible need of procuring the good of its brethren, especially their spiritual good, and the glory of God. In the mysterious colloquies He grants to her, the divine Master returns constantly to this subject. In the seventh chapter of the *Dialogue* the saint sets down these powerful words which find a remarkably profound echo in her own apostolic soul:

> So far as the soul loves Me, she loves her neighbor.... This is the means which I have given you, that you may exercise and prove your virtue therewith; because inasmuch as you can do Me no profit, you should do it to your neighbor. This proves that you possess Me by grace in your soul producing much fruit for your neighbor and making prayers to Me, seeking with sweet and amorous desire My honor and the salvation of souls.

The final result to which all interior effort tends and attains is the possession of God which is life everlasting. "In this way, therefore, she [the soul] reaches the term of her being, that is Myself, her God, who am Eternal Life. And these fruits cannot be taken from her without her will."

What is perhaps most characteristic in this conception of the interior life is the part played therein by the intellectual virtues and the predominance enjoyed by apostolic motives. The knowledge of self in God is the basis of the spiritual life. The virtue of discretion or supernatural prudence is its living rule. Having reached the end of her analysis, St. Catherine feels the need of declaring explicitly that the fruits produced by the tree of charity "are all flavored with discretion." As for the apostolic passion for the salvation of men and the glory of God, it is for our saint the very soul of the spiritual life. In all of this St. Catherine shows herself a worthy child of St. Dominic and the faithful disciple of St. Thomas.

II. The Knowledge of Self in God

We have just been studying the general idea of St. Catherine's conception of the spiritual life, the plan which, in her opinion, a Christian ought to follow in the work of his sanctification. The saint has summarized her thought on this point in a formula of characteristic verve such as proceeds only from the thought of a master: "Every perfection and every virtue proceeds from charity, and charity is nourished by humility, which results from the knowledge and holy hatred of self, that is, sensuality."[4]

Now we must take up each of the elements of this spiritual program, analyze it in detail, and finally clarify it sufficiently so that it may exert a serious influence upon our practical life. Let us begin with this *knowledge of self in God* which our saint lays down as the basis of the whole spiritual life, and let us try to describe its *nature*, its *fruit*, and the *means of acquiring it.*

🏛

Unfortunately, it is impossible to gather up and quote fully, in such a brief study, all the passages in her writings where St. Catherine defines the knowledge of self in God. It is a subject to which she returns constantly and which she develops with manifest enjoyment and extraordinary power. In the radiant ferment of her spiritual doctrine the

---

[4] *Dialogue*, chapter 63.

numerous pages she has devoted to it shine like divine luminaries of incomparable splendor. Since we must be resigned to making a selection, I shall cite only two passages which seem to me the most significant and comprehensive of all. I find the first in a letter from the saint to Cardinal Bonaventure of Padua:

> To this power of true and real virtue neither wealth nor rank nor worldly honor enable us to attain. It proceeds neither from high dignity nor from self-assurance, but solely from the knowledge the soul has of herself. Thanks to this knowledge, she sees that she does not exist by herself, but by reason of God. She recognizes her wretchedness and frailty, the time she has manifestly lost during which she might have accumulated precious gains. In this light, she acknowledges her unworthiness and her worth. Her unworthiness she perceives in the coarse envelope of her body which is the food of death, the food of worms, nothing but a sack of refuse. And yet we take greater pleasure in loving and satisfying that bag of putrefaction and indulging it, under the prompting of sensual love, than in the prosperity of the soul, which is nevertheless of so high a dignity that nothing excels it. For we see that God, impelled by His ardent charity, willed to create us, not in the state of irrational animals, nor in the likeness of the angels, but after His own image and likeness. To fulfill the achievement of His truth in us, that is to say, with a view to procuring us the end for which He created us and perfecting our dignity, He himself assumed our likeness when divinity was clothed in humanity. He restored grace to us, creating us anew in the blood of the sweet, loving Word, His only Son, who redeemed us not at the price of silver but with His blood. Therefore do the value of the blood He paid for us and the union of God with man manifest the ineffable love God has bestowed on us and the dignity we have received from our first creation, as has been said.[5]

In this admirable page, so full of realism and in a robust, outspoken style, almost daring in some places, without however ceasing to be entirely worthy of her, St. Catherine presents especially what the knowledge of self in God reveals to us about ourselves. The following is

---

[5] Letter T334.

another passage in which the saint defines essentially what this knowledge unfolds to us regarding God, explaining in particular, so to speak, His internal operation. It is therefore not a repetition of the preceding. The letter where it is to be found was addressed to Pope Urban VI:

> Most holy and sweetest Father in Christ, sweet Jesus, I, Catherine, servant and slave of the servants of Jesus Christ, write to you in His precious blood with the desire of seeing you established in a true light, so that, the eye of your intellect being enlightened, you may know and see the truth. For if you know it you will love it, and if you love it, virtues will shine forth in you. But what truth shall we know, most holy Father? We must know an eternal truth, a truth whereby we were loved before we existed. Whence shall we know it? From the knowledge of ourselves, seeing that God has created us in His image and likeness, urged thereunto by His ardent charity. This truth is that He created us to participate in Him and enjoy His eternal sovereign good. Who declared and manifested this truth to us? The blood of the humble, immaculate Lamb,... that blood in which, through a new creation, we have been restored to the life of grace. Who knows this truth? The soul who has divested herself of the cloud of self-love, the eye of the intellect being provided, by way of the pupil, with the light of holy faith.[6]

This is how, it seems to me, the doctrine formulated in these two passages may be interpreted so as to define the knowledge of self in God, its intimate nature and object. In the first place, this knowledge is the result of consideration on the part of our mind. "Open the eye of your intellect," our saint repeats constantly to her correspondents in the exhortations to self-knowledge which she addresses to them. But is our mere mind, unaided by any lights beyond its own, capable of so sublime a task? Let it be carefully observed that these natural lights of our intellect are useful, to a certain extent necessary, and already in themselves, precious graces on the part of God. St. Catherine never loses an opportunity for affirming this. Specifically, the admirable ninety-eighth chapter of the *Dialogue* should be re-read if one would learn what her thought is on this point; it is entitled: *How the light of reason is*

---

[6] Letter T305.

necessary to every soul that wishes to serve God in truth. Certainly our saint is not one who would signalize as priviledged candidates for Christian sanctity those souls in whom imagination and emotion predominate. But if these natural lights of our mind are requisite, they are not sufficient. Over and over again, St. Catherine explains that, in order to know oneself in God, one must have an intelligence enlightened by faith. In this eye of our intellect which she invites us to open wide upon ourselves and upon God there must be found, by way of the pupil, the supernatural virtue of faith, *holy faith*, as she calls it with so great and so justifiable a love.[7]

But upon what should it bear, this consideration of our intellect enlightened by faith, the result of which is to be a knowledge of ourselves in God? Upon an object which is not far to seek. It is quite close to us, within us; it is ourselves, our nothingness and unworthiness on the one hand, our natural and supernatural dignity on the other. But it must be well understood: St. Catherine does not wish us to stop with ourselves, to become absorbed in endless contemplation of what we are, what we are worth, for good or for ill. Especially is she the avowed enemy of those perpetual, minute, absorbing, anxious investigations into their defects and faults wherein certain excessively timid souls find satisfaction. She desires that from self-knowledge we should rise to the knowledge of God. On this point she has received an express declaration from her divine Master. "The soul," He tells her, "should season self-knowledge with that of My goodness, and the knowledge she has of Me with the knowledge of herself." Hence the saint requires insistently that, in our wretchedness, we learn to discover the goodness of God supplying for our indigence, the measureless love which inclines Him toward our lowliness. She likewise asks that we learn to recognize in our greatness for what it really is: the work and image of God, and a still further proof of the ardent love He bears us. It would appear that for our saint this two-fold contemplation of ourselves and of God should blend and become unified in the loving consideration of the mystery of Jesus, all together the most luminous proof possible of our misery as well as of our greatness and, above all, of the love God has for us.

⬆

---

[7] This notion of the close union between reason and faith is to be developed in Chapter VIII.

We have lingered somewhat over the definition of what St. Catherine means by the knowledge of self in God. Now we must speak of the fruits produced in the soul by this knowledge. The saint enumerates these precious effects and describes them in a letter to Pope Gregory XI:

> For the soul that knows itself humbles itself, because it sees nothing to be proud of; and ripens the sweet fruit of very ardent charity, recognizing in itself the unmeasured goodness of God; and aware that it is not, it attributes all its being to Him who Is. Whence, then, it seems that the soul is constrained to love what God loves and to hate what He hates. Oh, sweet and true knowledge, which does carry with you the knife of hate, and does stretch out the hand of holy desire, to draw forth and kill with this hate the worm of self-love—a worm that spoils and gnaws the root of our tree [the tree of charity], so that it cannot bear any fruit of life, but dries up, and its verdure lasts not![8]

As a contrast to this picture, may we be permitted to cite one more passage where St. Catherine presents the sad state of the soul bereft of this knowledge of self in God:

> Knowing neither Me nor himself, she [the soul] does not hate her own sensuality.[9] On the contrary, she loves it and seeks to satisfy all its desires. Thus she brings forth numerous mortal sins—like a woman who gives birth to still-born babes—nor does she love Me. Since she does not love Me, neither does she love what I love, namely, her neighbor; and she takes no pleasure in doing what pleases Me.[10]

---

[8] Letter T185; Scudder, p. 118. [The translation of the letters, whenever possible, is that of Vida Scudder, *Saint Catherine of Siena as Seen in her Letters* (New York: Dutton, 1927) which can be found on the internet. Scudder translated only 80 of Catherine's 381 letters; Suzanne Noffke, OP, has recently translated all of the letters. They are published in four volumes by the Arizona Center for Medieval and Renaissance Studies, Tempe, AZ].

[9] Like St. Thomas Aquinas, St. Catherine understands by *sensuality* the twofold sensitive appetite (concupiscible and irascible) which original sin withdrew from the control of reason while rendering it more susceptible.

[10] *Dialogue*, chapter 46.

As for the goods upon which the soul's self-love feeds, when she knows herself not in God, our saint characterizes their emptiness, ugliness and decrepitude in a few vigorous, almost brutal sentences which are nevertheless profoundly true, especially with the reservation she introduces therein. We will be forgiven for recalling, although this aspect of the matter is quite secondary when we are dealing with a Catherine of Siena, that it is a young woman of thirty who thus speaks:

> Oh, human blindness! Do you not see, unfortunate man, that you think to love things firm and stable, joyous things, good and fair? And they are mutable, the sum of wretchedness, hideous, and without any goodness; not as they are created things in themselves, since all are created by God, who is perfectly good, but through the nature of him who possesses them intemperately. How mutable are the riches and honors of the world in him who possesses them without God, without the fear of Him! For today is he rich and great, and tomorrow he is poor. How hideous is our bodily life, that living we shed stench from every part of our body! Simply a sack of dung, the food of worms, the food of death! Our life and the beauty of youth pass by, like the beauty of the flower when it is gathered from the plant. There is none who can save this beauty, none who can preserve it, that it be not taken, when it shall please the highest Judge to gather this flower of life by death; and none knows when.[11]

Humility, love of God and neighbor, hatred of self-love and sensuality, such are then the fruits of the knowledge of self in God. It would be desirable to be able to show all there is in this spiritual doctrine of true and profound psychology; but that would lead us too far afield. I admit frankly that I am in admiration at it. From the knowledge of our misery proceeds humility which is above all an exact estimate of what we are before God. The knowledge of God's goodness and of the measureless love He bears us and has evinced toward us by creating us, redeeming us, and in a thousand and one other ways, constrains us as it were to love Him and all that He loves, to render Him love for love. Finally, the realization that every evil in us springs from self-love, the ill-regulated love of ourselves, together with the love for God which has just been

---

[11] Letter to three Italian Cardinals; T310.

aroused or increased in our souls, enkindles a holy hatred therein so that we resolve courageously to destroy this internal enemy. Henceforth we are possessed of but one desire, to serve that God who loves us and whom we love, He whom the great poet Mistral, if we may be permitted to quote him here, calls "the God beautiful, the God who is our friend." Thus the knowledge of self in God establishes and develops in the soul possessed of it the divine energies demanded before all else for the progress of the spiritual life whose primary agents they are. It ensures the vitality and productivity of that precious tree which is charity whose fruits are all the Christian virtues.

⇧

One must not expect to find in St. Catherine of Siena a detailed statement of the practices to be observed in order to attain to this blessed knowledge of self in God. That does not enter into her plan. Perhaps it must even be admitted that neither her genius nor her grace incline her in that direction. We can nevertheless extract from her writings some brief indications of the series of acts demanded of a soul who desires to establish within herself this foundation of the spiritual life.

The first thing to be observed is that our saint considers the supernatural knowledge of oneself in God to be a special gift of grace. She sets down in her *Dialogue* these words of God the Father: "She [the soul] attributes to Me, through humility, the knowledge which she has obtained of herself, knowing that, by my grace, I have drawn her out of darkness and lifted her up into the light of true knowledge."[12] But the same grounds which impel the soul who has obtained this grace to give thanks for it also create the necessity of asking for it in one who still seeks to receive it. We ought, therefore above all to beseech God with humility and sincere desire to grant us the light we need that we may know Him in us and ourselves in Him.

Pursuing our research through the writings of the saint, we discover in several places this further indication: "Who knows this truth? The soul who has extricated herself from the cloud of self-love and possesses in her intellect the pupil of holy faith."[13] It is easy to recognize what St.

---

[12] *Dialogue*, chapter 7.

[13] Cf. *Dialogue*, chapters 45, 46, 51, etc.

Catherine means by this cloud of self-love from which the soul must free herself. She is certainly referring to those states in which, to a greater or less extent, the reason is darkened by that mist of passions and sense impressions arising from self-love and sensuality. If a man desires to apply himself to the knowledge of self in God he must absolutely disengage the intellect from this murky haze. But let us not be led astray. Our dear saint is far too wise and consistent to expect that at this stage of our spiritual life we can dispel with a single gesture and forever this unwholesome mist, or that we can therefore dry up the morass of sensuality and self-love whence it rises. That is precisely the role of the knowledge of self in God and of the ardent flame of charity it enkindles. The gust of wind following in the wake of a storm sweeps away the heavy black clouds, revealing in a limpid blue sky the great, radiant sun; nor does it on this account dry up the sea, the lakes and rivers which will one day form other clouds. Now our saint does not expect more from us. What she desires is that we should brush aside, if even for a moment, the cloud of self-love and, with recollection, gravity and sincerity, confront ourselves and God in the vast, true light of faith.

But all of this is still only a preparation. We must finally come to the point of that consideration, that meditation whose fruit is to be the knowledge of ourselves in God. We must apply our intelligence and our faith to considering the various objects the saint specified above, more particularly the mystery of Jesus which she characterized as the most convincing sign of our own misery and of the love God bears us. Our meditations will be profitably employed, even over a long period of time, in this consideration of what we are in relation to God and what God is in relation to us. We can likewise direct our examinations of conscience to this thought; they will thereby become a first-rate instrument in the work of our interior development.

Lastly, St. Catherine draws our attention to the part our very temptations may play, if we know how to use them, in the acquisition of this knowledge of ourselves in God. "One does not arrive at virtue," she writes, reporting the words of God, "except through knowledge of self, and knowledge of Me, which knowledge is more perfectly acquired in the time of temptation, because then man knows himself to be nothing, being unable to lift off himself the pains and vexations which he would flee; and he knows Me in his will, which is fortified by my goodness, so that it does not yield to these thoughts."[14] The truth of these divine words appears clearly to all those who have experienced such states, and there is no one who has not undergone something of the sort.

⇡

The intimate nature of the knowledge of self in God, its effects and the means of acquiring it: these I have tried to explain in the light of St. Catherine of Siena. I do not believe I have said anything original and I am glad to have it so. On the other hand, I cannot claim to have brought to light and made use of all that the writings of our saint contain on this subject. Let it be recalled that these studies are not calculated to replace the direct reading of the saint's works but only to facilitate it and make it more profitable. The teaching we have presented is assuredly elevated. Yet it is so profoundly true and, in a word, so succinct and clear that it is difficult to believe any souls of good will should not find food therein proportionate to their need. May God deign to give us all a perfect understanding of it and the grace to conform our lives thereto.

III. Humility

The teachings of St. Catherine on humility are scattered through her *Dialogue* and letters, more especially the latter. She formulated them according to needs and occasions or again in proportion to the lights received from God in her ecstasies. Never did she set herself the task of analyzing this virtue basically so as to give us a complete theory regarding it. To arrive at such a theory we are reduced to the necessity of assembling the fragmentary explanations she has left to us.

Like a painstaking and able craftsman, St. Catherine has cut the very delicate stones from which the mosaic is to be composed. It is up to us to put them together according to their connections, to complete the unfinished work of art, and the divine lineaments of humility, as envisaged by our saint, will stand forth. Perhaps in detail and in certain spots the outlines will appear somewhat vague, indefinite and hazy. But the essential lines will only be more striking on this account. A mystical figure, wrapped in infinite grace and compelling sweetness, as conceived

---

[14] *Dialogue*, chapter 43.

by the Sienese primitives in their artistic contemplation, she will appeal to our hearts even more than to our eyes. St. Catherine will teach us how to reproduce the features of this attractive model in our souls.

⇧

What our saint emphasizes from the beginning with reference to humility is the close bond of dependence linking it to self-knowledge. "Humility proceeds from self-knowledge."[15] And in a letter to Monna Alessa of Siena she clothes the same thought in an attractive metaphor: "From such knowledge flows the stream of humility."[16]

But how does this knowledge of ourselves produce humility in us? St. Catherine explains it herself. Let us follow with gentle patience the development, rather slow at this point, of her analysis. She writes to Master Andrea di Vanni descended from an illustrious family of painters and himself an artist and a captain of the people of Siena: "Where does he find it [humility]? In the cell of self-knowledge... He, in fact, who knows himself finds nothing of which he can be proud. That which is not can scarcely arrive at pride."[17] To Don Robert of Naples she speaks in even more explicit terms: "When the soul realizes that she is not, that, moreover, she does that which is not, namely evil and sin, she suddenly becomes humble before God and every creature for the sake of God."[18] In a charming letter to her niece Nanna, a very young girl, our saint adds a few more details. She has just explained at length and with delicate, almost subtle artistry the Gospel parable of the wise virgins. She describes the lamp whose light must illumine them while they wait, without knowing the hour, of the bridegroom's return. The flame of divine charity burns therein and the brightness of this flame is the light of holy faith. But in the lamp which is our soul there must be oil and precisely they, among the virgins, are wise who have provided themselves with a good supply of it.

> By oil is meant that sweet little virtue, profound humility: for it is fitting that the bride of Christ be humble and gentle and

---

15 *Dialogue*, chapter 9.

16 Letter T49; Scudder, p. 27.

17 Letter T366.

18 Letter T342.

patient... But we cannot attain this virtue of humility except by true knowledge of ourselves, knowing our misery and frailty, and that we by ourselves can do no good deed, nor escape any conflict or pain; for if we have a bodily infirmity, or a pain or conflict in our minds, we cannot escape it or remove it—for if we could we should escape from it swiftly. So it is quite true that we in ourselves are nothing other than infamy, misery, stench, frailty, and sins; wherefore, we ought always to abide low and humble.[19]

How simple, kind, gracious and genuinely motherly St. Catherine shows herself to be in this letter to her niece! Is it not admirable and especially touching to find a saint who had penetrated so deeply into the mysteries of God and of His Christ confining herself to such simple, ordinary experiences? We seem to catch her smiling as she dictates this letter with a good-natured smile barely tinged with an imperceptible and gentle playfulness. However young she might have been, Nanna must have grasped this plain, homespun spirituality, finding it applicable to her unpretentious childhood experiences. Of all her aunt's remarks, the one who is most priminant in this passage must have gained from her a very prompt acquiescence: "if we could we should escape from it [any of these trials, that is] swiftly."

But it is time to extract the essential idea from these various fragments. It may be stated thus: self-knowledge leads us to the conviction that, of ourselves, we are nothing, are worth nothing, and can do nothing. In all truth, according to the word of the Father to St. Catherine, "we are they who are not." As a consequence the only attitude which becomes us, at least insofar as our mind is concerned, and which corresponds to what we are, is one of humility. Self-knowledge is therefore the source of humility inasmuch as it furnishes us with the necessary motives, imposes them upon us, overwhelms us with their evidence. It becomes, for our intellect, the basis of humility its measure and its rule.

Strictly speaking, however, a knowledge of our nothingness is not humility. To find this virtue we must descend from the mind into the heart and there trace the influence of the conviction we hold regarding our nothingness, the judgment we pass upon ourselves. Only there shall

---

[19] Letter T23; Scudder, pp. 54-55.

we encounter that combination of dispositions and moral inclinations which constitute humility.

One of the passages which best reveal St. Catherine's conception of it is found in this letter to Monna Alessa of which we have already spoken.

> From such knowledge flows the stream of humility; which never seizes on any mere report [scandal], nor takes offence at anything, but bears every insult, every loss of consolation, and every sorrow, from whatever direction they may come, patiently, with joy. Shame appears as glory, and great persecutions refreshment; and it rejoices in all, seeing itself punished for that perverse law of self-will in its members which forever rebels against God; and it sees itself conformed with Christ Jesus crucified, the way and the doctrine of truth.[20]

From all this highly particularized psychology through which humility develops, the radical element, the one we must retain is this: never does the humble soul seek a reputation, never does she desire to be esteemed as of any account, since in reality and in her own judgment, of herself she is nothing.

Nevertheless, the following extract from a letter of the saint to Monna Agnesa, widow of the Sienese Orso Malavolti, offers us an additional element: "O my most sweet daughter, learn from this virgin Saint Agnes [of Montepulciano] humility. She sought unceasingly to abase herself, subjecting herself for God's sake to every creature and acknowledging that it was from God she drew every grace and virtue. Thus did she preserve within her the virtue of humility."[21] Not only does the humble soul not seek esteem, but in all things, with all her might, she abases herself. This inclination to lowliness she satisfies by subjecting herself for God's sake to every creature and by attributing to God all that she may possess of grace and virtue.

St. Catherine indicates two more dispositions which, without being humility itself, since our saint calls them "handmaids of humility," are intimately associated with it. They fill in with still greater precision the portrait of that virtue. These dispositions are self-disgust and what our

---

[20] Letter T49; Scudder, p. 27.

[21] Letter T61.

saint terms *viltà*, a word difficult to translate but implying a profound sense of one's lowliness [vileness].

⇧

Humility, then, consists of a profound conviction in the mind of our own nothingness, and, in the heart, of the intention not to seek esteem, an inclination to abase ourselves. Hence, to become humble, we must develop within us that conviction and inclination. Let us inquire of our saint what are, in her judgment, the means best adapted to this end.

Since the conviction of our nothingness is the natural result of self-knowledge, the whole question resolves itself, on this point, into the necessity for knowing ourselves as we really are; and since we have already indicated in the preceding chapter the means of attaining it, there is no need to repeat the matter here. That leaves us free to introduce in this second part some considerations which had to be omitted in the former study. From the practical point of view they are of the greatest importance.

Our saint distinguishes clearly between humility and an inward sense of shame. Shame or confusion leads to discouragement and is quite the opposite of a virtue. Nevertheless, according to St. Catherine, it is in confusion rather than humility that self-knowledge terminates if it is not isolated. "Knowledge of self requires to be seasoned with knowledge of Me, lest it bring the soul to confusion."[22] If we aim at having the knowledge of our nothingness, misery, and impotence lead us to humility, it must be completed and set off by a knowledge of God's love for us, of His gifts to us. St. Catherine clearly presupposes this since, while praising the humility of St. Agnes of Montepulciano, she remarks that this humble virgin attributed to God alone all that she perceived in herself of graces and virtues. She therefore knew that there was in her something beyond nothingness and misery—the precious gifts of God. Far from ignoring or denying the good that is in us on God's account, humility demands that we recognize it; otherwise it would lose its character of virtue and become a depressing confusion. But this good which she discovers within her, the humble soul attributes to God alone;

---

[22] *Dialogue*, chapter 73.

119

acknowledging it, she plunges even more profoundly into the sense of her nothingness.

The manner in which St. Catherine describes humility suggests still another observation which completes the characterization of this self-knowledge which we must first acquire in order to become humble. This nothingness, this moral misery and impotence of which St. Catherine speaks and of which she desires us to become aware, is perhaps less our own faults in detail, our personal wretchedness, than the misery of humanity as it exists in us. She constantly reverts in her writings to the nonentity of the creature, the baseness and powerlessness of human nature. In our personal faults it is the visible manifestation of this fallen nature that she urges us to discover; it is of this she would have us well persuaded. The conviction on which, in her opinion, humility should rest, has nothing in common with the fear that obsesses certain timorous souls regarding their personal impotence or powerlessness. Assuredly St. Catherine wishes us to be conscious of this latter, since it is there that our nothingness as creatures and our misery as men are veiled to us in a concrete, tangible way. But she will not have us remain shut up therein. We must reach out to be something much deeper and more universal, more persuasive and less disturbing, to the conviction that, insofar as we are creatures we are nonentity and powerless; that insofar as we are men and fallen men, we are misery and sin.

There is one fact which cannot fail to impress us when we read St. Catherine's writings and study her personal life. The humility she teaches and practices is at once profound, essential, absolute and based upon truth, as far removed from illusion as from scrupulosity; it is broad and acceptable. The two observations we have just considered throw light upon this mystery. They will also guide us in the acquisition of that self-knowledge and that humility of which it is the source.

But it is not enough to be convinced of one's misery in order to be humble. Our intellect may very well recognize in humility the only true attitude for us to assume, while our will remains reluctant, even rebellious. This attitude which we recognize as true must also appear to us as good. Only the good is capable of moving our heart, and since it is after all in the heart that humility is to be found, it must be won over by revealing that virtue to it as good and beneficial. St. Catherine has taken the trouble to indicate for us the means best calculated to produce in our heart, on behalf of humility, that attraction which it feels toward what is good and beneficent. She takes this stand decisively in a letter to the Countess Giovanna di Mileto et di Terra Nuova: "Love Him [God] and serve Him with all your heart and all your strength, without reserve, with true and very deep humility, loving your neighbor as yourself. But you will say to me: How can I acquire this humility? I feel myself to be full of self-love, inclined toward every act of pride."[23] Here is the great practical problem presented. Let us hear St. Catherine's reply; it is of interest to others beside the Countess Giovanna.

> I answer that if you are willing, by means of divine grace you will very promptly despoil yourself [of self-love and pride], and this grace is given to him who desires it. This is how. By means of the light, consider the humility of God.... it appears so profound that it exceeds man's comprehension. Has anything like it ever been seen in a creature? Assuredly not. Is there anything greater than to see God humiliated to the level of man, the supreme Excellence reduced to such lowliness, clothed in our humanity, God living visibly among men, bearing our infirmities, our poverty and wretchedness? He humbled Himself even to the shameful death of the cross. Immensity became little, to the confusion of those who are inflated with pride, who ever seek to be greatest. They do not realize that they are descending to the lowest baseness and misery. Thus we find the spring of humility pouring forth from Him.

To consider the humility of God in Jesus is therefore, in the mind of St. Catherine, the first means of persuading our heart of the value of humility. Since God has given us the example, we cannot fail to recognize that it is good and salutary to be humble. The desire to be conformed to Jesus Christ cannot help but induce us to practice humility. It is undeniable that the saint has seen the matter in the right light. In fact it is certainly this haunting thought of the humility of God in Jesus which has produced in the saints a tremendous, insatiable need for self-abasement. St. Catherine had personally experienced the efficacy of this means which she recommends: "O my soul, alas! You have wasted all the time of thy life; it is on this account that so many scourges and evils have come upon the world and the holy Church;" if she is humble to the extent

---

[23] Letter T345.

of uttering such words as these, it is because the thought of the humility of Jesus spurs her on unceasingly.

The second means of winning over our heart to humility is to consider, as St. Catherine invites us to do, the effects of this virtue or, more accurately, its benefits.

> Dearest daughter in Christ sweet Jesus: I Catherine servant and slave of the servants of Jesus Christ, write to you in His precious Blood, with desire to see you clothed in true and perfect humility—for that is a little virtue which makes us great in the sweet sight of God. This is the virtue which constrained and inclined God to make His most sweet Son incarnate in the womb of Mary. It is as exalted as the proud are humbled; it shines in the sight of God and men; it binds the hands of the wicked, it unites the soul with God, it purifies and washes away the soil of our sin, and calls on God to show us mercy.[24]

Elsewhere the saint very often declares that humility is the sole breeding ground of divine charity in our souls, the soil in which this divine tree must be planted lest it wither away. If we meditate on all of this, it is not likely that our heart should remain unmoved by the desire for humility or negligent in its practice.

⇑

In conclusion, let us hearken to the voice of God lamenting over the pride of men and the ravages it works in their souls in which it kills the divine life.

> I have made them trees of love [God says to St. Catherine] with the life of grace which they received in Holy Baptism; and they have become trees of death, because they are dead, as I have already said to thee. Do you know how this tree finds such roots? In the height of pride, which is nourished by their own sensitive self-love. Its branch is their own impatience, and its offshoot indiscretion: these are the four principal vices which destroy the soul of him who is a tree of death... Inside the tree is nourished the worm of conscience [remorse], which, while man lives in mortal sin, is blinded by self-love, and therefore

---

[24] Letter T340; Scudder, p. 71.

felt but little; the fruits of this tree are mortal, for they have drawn their nourishment, which should have been humility, from the roots of pride, and the miserable soul is full of ingratitude, whence proceeds every evil.[25]

IV. Charity

The knowledge of self in God as well as humility are still only a preparation for the true divine life, in the judgment of St. Catherine. Charity alone, the vital seed sown in the very depths of our souls by the Holy Spirit, contains life, eternal life. Christian discipline, especially this progress in the knowledge of ourselves and of God, this enlightened cultivation of humility which the saint has so urgently recommended: these have no other object but to insure the growth and development in us of divine charity.

It is supremely important, then, for us to know what charity is, to ponder over the benefits of which it is the source, to learn the means of increasing it within us and the right way to practice it. St. Catherine will teach us this. In this matter above all she is an incomparable guide. Let us sit at the feet of our Mother, as the disciples whom she loved were wont to do, and may our attentive, affectionately docile souls lose nothing of her teaching.

⚜

"What is charity?" our dear saint asks in a letter to the Countess Benedetta Salimbeni of Siena. "It is an ineffable love..."[26] It is not an external attitude which one assumes, words or phrases before which one bows, in which one is swathed, so to speak. It is not even, primarily at least, certain practices or acts. Essentially, charity is a sentiment of the heart, an affection of the will. St. Catherine has said it: "It is a love," that word says all that needs to be said without any commentary.

But what is the object of this love, this ineffable love? What do we love, what ought we to love by charity? The saint explains in the following terms to Don Giovanni, a monk of Vallombrosa: "By charity

---

[25] *Dialogue*, chapter 31,

[26] Letter T113.

man forgets himself. He does not seek himself for his own sake but for God's. He loves God for God's sake, knowing that He is the sovereign, eternal Goodness and worthy of being loved."[27] Hence primary and, in a sense, the unique object of charity is God. Him alone do we love in Himself and for Himself, because He alone is sovereign Goodness. If we love something else together with Him, as in fact we do and should do, namely ourselves in the first place and then our neighbor, it is because of Him and for Him. In ourselves and in our neighbor it is still God whom we love, the traces of His sovereign, eternal Goodness, the reflection of His supreme Beauty, the gifts and purposes of His love and, so to speak, that very love itself wherewith He honors His creature. Hence that identity, surprising at first sight, between the love of God and the love of neighbor—and we may add, the legitimate love of self—which St. Catherine asserts in the following words, dictated by the eternal Father: "Love of Me and of her neighbor are one and the same thing, and, so far as the soul loves Me, she loves her neighbor, because love towards him issues from Me."[28]

If we pass from this general definition to a study of the concrete forms under which charity presents itself, we find that St. Catherine has subtly analyzed its two principal degrees: the imperfect, self-seeking love of God and perfect, disinterested charity. With regard to the former, she writes in her *Dialogue*:

> Some there are who have become faithful servants, serving Me with fidelity without servile fear of punishment, but rather with love. This very love, however, if they serve Me with a view to their own profit, or the delight and pleasure which they find in Me, is imperfect. Do you know what proves the imperfection of this love? The withdrawal of the consolations which they found in Me, and the insufficiency and short duration of their love for their neighbor, which grows weak by degrees, and often disappears. Towards Me their love grows weak when, on occasion, in order to exercise them in virtue and raise them above their imperfection, I withdraw from their minds My consolation and allow them to fall into battles and perplexities... At such a time these weak ones, of whom I speak,

---

[27] Letter T322.

[28] *Dialogue*, chapter 7.

relax their energy, impatiently turning backwards, and sometimes abandon, under color of virtue, many of their exercises saying to themselves, *This labor does not profit me.* All this they do, because they feel themselves deprived of mental consolations.[29]

To this imperfect, self-seeking charity, mingled with spiritual self-love, St. Catherine sets up in contrasts perfect charity. This is no longer the love of servants and hirelings but of the children of God. The voice of our saint, just now reluctant and tinged with sadness, becomes impregnated with serene happiness, animated, joyfully singing:

> But when the soul has become a child of God, that is, when she finds herself established in perfect charity, then she acts like a real son who never ceases to love his father, loving him not with a mercenary love that looks to the advantage he thus obtains, and fears to offend him from the dread of punishment, but solely because he is good, is his father, and from the attraction of his very nature. It is this nature itself, deriving from the love of his father, which gives him strength; it is the love his father bears him which urges him to love and serve that father. One may therefore say of him that he is truly a son. I affirm then that our love for the heavenly Father ought to consist in loving Him not with a view to any personal profit or fear of punishment, but solely because He is the sovereign Being, eternally good with an infinite Goodness and worthy of being loved, whereas nothing else deserves our love apart from God. For His sake we must love and serve every creature. That is the love of the Father.[30]

That is indeed true charity. Doubtless, imperfect, self-seeking love is good, praiseworthy and meritorious. It is no small thing to be a faithful servant of God. But only disinterested love, the love of God divested of an egoistic reference to self, can make of us true sons of the heavenly Father. It is to that we are called, tenderly urged by the love God bears us; to what we must tend with humility and perseverance.

⚜

---

[29] *Dialogue*, chapter 60.

[30] Letter to Queen Joanna of Naples; T133.

There is perhaps no single one of the virtues which are the support of our Christian life, not one of the gifts and merits which constitutes our spiritual treasure which St. Catherine does not ascribe to charity. Among all these benefits of charity we can indicate here only the more important and more characteristic.

The love of God inspires us with a keen sense of regret and repulsion for sin; this is probably how it begins to make its influence felt. In a letter of the saint to Messer Ristoro Canigiani, one of the supporters of the Guelph party in Florence, we read the following:

> Charity is so mild that it leaves no room for bitterness, at least of the kind which saddens the soul. But it produces a very gentle dissatisfaction upon which the soul may feed. This consists of a true knowledge of self wherein the soul sees the past and presents faults of which she has been guilty before her Creator. Such knowledge becomes the source of real grief in her. She is pained by the thought of having offended this sovereign, eternal Good, of having besmirched the fair countenance of her soul, washed in the blood of the humble, immaculate Lamb.[31]

Under the domination of this loving regret, the soul conceives an energetic hatred of that sensual self-love wherein she sees the origin and cause of all evil. "Oh, sweet and glorious fire [of charity]," she exclaims, "which is of such power that it quenches fire, and every inordinate delight and pleasure and all love of self!" Then suddenly changing her metaphor, she adds: "This love is like a drop of water, which is swiftly consumed in the furnace!"[32]

However, charity is not content with destroying the last vestiges of sin in us, with striving to extinguish its flame. As the seed and well-spring of divine life, it diffuses and develops life.

> Sweet charity, O beloved mother, you give birth to all the virtues which are your daughters. Learn, my very dear sister, that without charity there is no living virtue. That is what was said by St. Paul the vessel of election whose soul was possessed

---

[31] Letter T289.

[32] Letter to Gregory XI; T185; Scudder, p. 120.

by love: "If I speak with the tongues of men and of angels...if I should give all my goods to the poor...and have not charity, it profits me not." That is the truth. For the soul who is not in charity can do nothing that is pleasing to God. The fruits of her virtues are dead. Why are they dead? Because God, that is charity, is not there to give them life. For he who is in charity is in God and God in him.[33]

The very dear sister to whom St. Catherine addressed such lofty theological teaching was Monna Pavola, a Sienese residing at Fiesole.

"He is in God and God in him." These words lead us to point out another effect of charity, perhaps the highest, but at any rate one of those whereby the intimate nature of this virtue is best revealed. Charity, St. Catherine tells us, is a love. We shall see that these are not mere words.

By desire and affection, and union of love, [God] makes her [who loves Him] another Himself. Christ would seem to have meant this, when He said: *To him who will love Me and will observe My commandment, will I manifest Myself; and he shall be one thing with Me and I with him.* In several places we find similar words, by which we can see that it is indeed, through the effect of love, that the soul becomes another Himself. That this may be seen more clearly, I will mention what I remember having heard from a handmaid of God, namely, that when she was lifted up in prayer, with great elevation of mind, God was not wont to conceal from the eye of her intellect, the love which He had for His servants, but rather to manifest it; and, that among other things, He used to say: "Open the eye of your intellect, and gaze into the beauty of My rational creature. And look at those creatures who, among the beauties which I have given to the soul, creating her in My image and likeness, are clothed with the nuptial garment (that is, the garment of love), adorned with many virtues, by which they are united with Me through love. And yet I tell you, if you should ask Me, who these are, I should reply (said the sweet and amorous Word of God) "they are another Myself, inasmuch as they have lost and denied their own will, and are clothed with mine, are united to

---

[33] Letter T97.

mine, are conformed to mine." It is therefore true, indeed, that the soul unites herself with God by the affection of love.[34]

If it is true that through charity the soul and God are united until they form but one, so close is their union of love, we shall not be astonished to find in St. Catherine's writings this new and final characteristic: "As soon as the soul has found and tasted this very sweet love...she is most eager to follow in every respect the example and ways of Him whom she loves."[35]

Keen regret for having offended God, but without depressing sadness or discouragement, culminating in an energetic hatred for the inordinate self-love to which these faults are to be imputed; all the other virtues enkindled, re-vivified, rendered meritorious, henceforth bearing fruits of life eternal; the most intimate union of love between God and the soul so as henceforth to form but one and, as supreme consequence, the intense desire the soul experiences of becoming entirely like unto the God she loves, imitating His conduct and adopting His ways; such, according to the spiritual teaching of St. Catherine, are the effects proper to charity. All of this is extremely remarkable for its theological precision and richness as well as its psychological insight and truth.

⇧

If we now inquire as to the means of attaining to the love of God and the right way of practicing charity, we shall find in St. Catherine all the light to be wished for.

In a letter to the Countess Benedetta Salimbeni, our saint presents and resolves the first of these two questions:

> But you will say, my beloved daughter: What way must I follow to find and acquire this love? Here is my answer: Love is acquired by means of light. In fact, one does not know what one does not see. Consequently, not being known it is not loved. You must therefore possess the light which will enable you to see and know what you ought to love. Since light is

---

[34] *Dialogue*, chapter 1.

[35] Letter to Cardinal Giacomo Orsini; T101.

indispensable to us, God has provided for this necessity by giving us the light of the intellect which is the noblest part of the soul; and in this intellect He has placed the pupil of most holy faith... We ought to open the eyes of the intellect in the light of most holy faith and take as its object the incalculable love God has shown toward us. Then the heart, perceiving this love, will not be able to help loving Him who the intellect sees and truly knows.[36]

The saint goes so far as to establish a proportion between the perfection of this supernatural knowledge and the perfection of charity:

The more that, opening the eye of the intellect, you apply yourself to a consideration of the center, the abyss of measureless charity God has for you, the love He has shown for you through the Word, His Son, the more you will feel impelled to love, to love sincerely, with all your heart, all your affection and all your might, generously, unselfishly, without any concern for your personal advantage. You see, indeed, that God loves you for your own good and not for His, for He is our God and has no need of us. By the same token, you, like every rational creature, ought to love God for God's sake, insofar as He is the sovereign and eternal Good, not with a view to your personal profit, and your neighbor for His sake.[37]

She goes even further in the following passage from the *Dialogue*, where she reports the express words of God: "He who know more loves Me more... and if you should ask Me, whether one who has no knowledge can attain to this love, I should reply, yes it is possible that he may attain to it, but an individual case does not make a general law and I always discourse to you in general."[38] The general law, by which alone we can regulate our conduct, is therefore to seek the means of acquiring charity, preserving it and making progress therein from an ever more perfect knowledge, a constantly renewed meditation on God's love for us.

---

[36] Letter T113.

[37] Letter to Pietro Venture of Siena; T47.

[38] *Dialogue*, chapter 131.

The love God bears toward us is then what we must know and ponder. This is another aspect of our saint's doctrine. Basically, knowledge is but a means of subjecting ourselves to the influence of this love of God. What really touches our heart and produces in us that appeal of love, which St. Catherine tells us it is impossible to resist, is the very love of God for us, that divine charity whose reality, gratuity, and unspeakable excess are borne in upon our thought. Love is derived from love, enkindled by love, Catherine repeats over and over without ever wearying. Speaking, alas, of a quite different love, Dante had already adverted to: "Love that exempts no one beloved from loving."[39] What, then, is the reason for this mysterious power? Here is her beautiful reply:

> The heart of man is in no wise so drawn as by love, because he was made by love. This seems to be the reason why he loves so much, that he was made by nothing but love, both his soul and his body. For by love God created him in His image and likeness, and by love his father and mother gave him substance, conceiving and bearing a son.[40]

One final word and we shall have all the essentials of St. Catherine's teaching regarding the acquisition of charity and progress in this virtue. She has already told us above that God had manifested His love for us through the Word, His Son. In other passages she clarifies this idea. "Because [man] knows the truth about God from seeing the ineffable love He shows through the blood of His Son,... it would seem that he cannot and, in fact, he cannot cease loving his Creator as long as he perseveres in this knowledge." The blood of Jesus poured forth for us is the evidence, eloquent beyond all others, of the love God bears us. It is therefore, above all, with this mystery that the meditations should be concerned wherein St. Catherine assures us that we shall find and draw forth charity. She bursts forth into a splendid hymn of thanksgiving in honor of this blood, the dazzling proof of God's love, the furnace where our charity is enkindled: "O Blood... you burn and consume the soul in the glowing fire of divine charity... You envelope her in the flames of divine charity, for she cannot taste you, O Blood, without being wrapped

---

[39] *Inferno*, Canto V, verse 103 (Longfellow's translation).

[40] Letter to Gregory XI; T196; Scudder, p. 126.

and clothed in flames. It is, indeed amid the flames of love that you were poured out....."[41]

As for the manner of evincing our love of God, of practicing charity, St. Catherine's teachings are no less precise and characteristic. I shall limit myself to citing this passage from a letter to Benuccio di Piero and Bernardo di Misser Uberto de Belforti, two gentlemen of Volterra.

> But I desire that you know that one cannot love God... except by means of one's neighbor. Why? I shall tell you. I cannot give evidence of the love I have for my Creator directly to Him. It is impossible to render any service to God. It is proper, therefore, to have recourse to a creature as an intermediary, to come to the aid of a creature and render him those services which I cannot render to God.

Then, making use of the dialogue between Jesus and St. Peter as reported in St. John's gospel, she gives this very apt commentary on it: "That is why Christ, addressing St. Peter, asks him: *Simon, do you love Me?* Upon receiving an affirmative reply, Christ adds: *Feed My sheep.* This love you have for Me can do Me no good. Do good, therefore, to your neighbor."[42]

Among the touching exhortations to the love of God which we read in St. Catherine of Siena, the following, perhaps the most discreet in tone and most human in inspiration, has forced itself upon my mind as a fitting conclusion to this chapter. It is God Himself who speaks:

> Do you love beauty? I am Beauty. Do you love goodness? I am Goodness, being sovereignly good. I am Wisdom. I am the gentle, just, merciful God. I am magnanimous knowing no avarice. I am He who gives to whoever asks of Me, opens to whoever knocks with sincerity, responds to whoever calls upon Me. I am not insensible, but grateful, intending to reward him who spends himself for My sake, for the glory and praise of My name. I am joy and I establish in supreme joy the soul who

---

[41] Letter to Stefano Maconi; T195.

[42] Letter T103.

clothes herself in My will. I am that sovereign Providence who never fails My servants."[43]

V. Discernment

In the spiritual doctrine of St. Catherine what is called *"la santa virtu della discrezione"* plays a preeminent part. Unfortunately, this word *discretion,* suggests in English as well as French, primarily the idea of reserve in speech and conduct, which is not the characteristic element of *"la discrezione"* as Catherine understands it. The word *discernment,* although somewhat vague, is perhaps closer to her thought.

This latter is more or less summarized in two passages from her writings, chapters nine to eleven of the *Dialogue* and a letter to Sister Daniella of Orvieto.[44] I do not think she has explained herself quite so systematically with regard to any other point of her spiritual teaching. She has what amounts to a theory about discernment or discretion. It will suffice for us to combine the data furnished by these two documents, sifting out certain accidental traits and setting in relief the essential lines, so as to obtain a clear picture, a living portrait of this virtue, dear above all to St. Catherine. Moreover, in this portrait it is the very countenance of her own soul which will shine forth under one of its most personal aspects, one which has perhaps not always been sufficiently noticed.

⬆

According to her wont, St. Catherine is first of all concerned with indicating the place occupied by discretion in our spiritual organism, discovering its vital connections or, as she calls them, its roots. Is this not the best means of discovering the spiritual forces and virtues which unite to constitute it, expanding so as to produce it? Furthermore, is it not taking the most direct and the surest road which leads to the very heart of this complex virtue? She writes, then, to Sister Daniella of Orvieto:

---

[43] *Dialogue,* chapter 141.

[44] Letter T213; Scudder, p. 144.

Dearest daughter and sister in Christ sweet Jesus: I Catherine, servant and slave of the servants of Jesus Christ, write to you in His precious Blood, with desire to see in you the holy virtue of discretion, which it is necessary for us to have if we wish to be saved. Why is it so necessary? Because it proceeds from the knowledge of ourselves and of God; in this house its roots are planted. It is really an offspring of charity, which, properly speaking, is discretion—and illumined knowledge which the soul has, as I said, of God and itself.[45]

In the *Dialogue* the saint emphasizes the role of humility in the genesis of discretion. Let us meekly accept the complicated and, apparently, rather hesitant development of her allegory.

This virtue of discretion [God the father declares to Catherine] is no other than a true knowledge which the soul should have of herself and of Me, and in this knowledge is virtue rooted. Discretion is the only child of self-knowledge, and wedding with charity, has indeed many other branches; but that which gives life to the tree, to its branches, and its root, is the ground of humility, in which it is planted, which humility is the foster-mother and nurse of charity, by whose means this tree remains in the perpetual calm of discretion. Because otherwise the tree would not produce the virtue of discretion, or any fruit of life, if it were not planted in the virtue of humility, because humility proceeds from self-knowledge. And I have already said to you, that the root of discretion is a real knowledge of self and of My goodness.[46]

It appears to me that Catherine's thought can be summarized in this formula: Discretion is the knowledge of self in God, no longer under its initial form or in its native state, but developed in humility and vivified by charity. However this is still only a general definition. Let us try to grasp what pertains strictly to discretion, constituting and characterizing it as a special virtue.

Speaking of a soul in whom discretion has begun to make its influence felt, St. Catherine writes to Daniella: "The chief thing it does is this:

---

[45] Ibid.

[46] *Dialogue*, chapter 9.

having seen, in a reasonable light, what it ought to render and to whom, it renders this with perfect discretion at once." The *Dialogue* expresses the same idea in even more concise terms: "The soul immediately, and discreetly, renders to each one his due."[47] The essential act of the virtue of discretion, revealing to us its proper nature, is therefore to cause us to see what we owe to each one and incline us to render it to him by the appropriate means. Let us allow the saint to explain herself in some detail. Who are these debtors of ours and what can it be that we owe them?

> Chiefly to Me [she hears God say to her] in rendering praise and glory to My Name, and in referring to Me the graces and the gifts which she sees and knows she has received from Me; and rendering to herself that which she sees herself to have merited, knowing that she does not even exist of herself, and attributing to Me, and not to herself, her being, which she knows she has received by grace from Me, and every other grace which she has received besides. And she seems to herself to be ungrateful for so many benefits, and negligent, in that she has not made the most of her time, and the graces she has received, and so seems to herself worthy of suffering; wherefore she becomes odious and displeasing to herself through her guilt.

A little further on she resumes and completes this analysis:

> Contrariwise those who possess the virtue discretion. For, when they have rendered what is due to Me and to themselves, they proceed to render to their neighbor their principal debt of love, and of humble and continuous prayer, which all should pay to each other, and further, the debt of doctrine, and example of a holy and honorable life, counseling and helping others according to their needs for salvation.[48]

Manifestly, we find once more at the very heart of the virtue of discretion that knowledge of self and of God upon which St. Catherine bases the whole of the spiritual life. But discretion is no longer that bare knowledge of what we are in relation to God and of what God is in

---

[47] Ibid.

[48] Ibid.

relation to us. While founded upon this knowledge, it is a positive, practical appreciation, all prepared to become a rule of conduct, of our condition and of the burdens which weigh upon us, our debts, as Catherine declares, what we owe to God, to our neighbor, and to ourselves. This is something really new.

With this just appreciation of what we owe to everyone, the proper effect of discretion, St. Catherine, in accordance with a device which is familiar to her, contrasts the disorder of thought and action which reveals the absence of this virtue. The letter to Daniella contains some very significant developments of this point. The soul possessed of the virtue of discretion

> Renders to God His due of honor—not like an indiscreet robber, who wants to give honor to himself, and, seeking his own honor and pleasure, does not mind insulting God and harming his neighbor. When the roots of inclination in the soul are rotted by indiscretion, all its works, relating to others or to itself, are rotten. All relating to others, I say: for it imposes burdens indiscreetly, and lays down the law to other people, seculars or spiritual, or of whatever rank they may be. If such a person admonishes or advises, he does it indiscreetly, and wants to load everyone else with the burden which he carries himself.

A parallel passage of the *Dialogue* also deserves to be cited.

> Were this humility not in the soul, the soul would be indiscreet, indiscretion being founded on pride, as discretion is on humility. An indiscreet soul robs Me of the honor due to Me, and attributes it to herself, through vainglory, and that which is really her own she imputes to Me, grieving and murmuring concerning My mysteries, with which I work in her soul and in those of My other creatures; wherefore everything in Me and in her neighbor is cause of scandal to her.[49]

It seems to me that all of this authorizes us to declare: possession of the virtue of discernment or discretion means, in the spiritual life, having

---

[49] Ibid.

135

judgment. The pre-requisite virtues which cooperate and tend to form this spiritual judgment in us are the knowledge of self in God, humility and charity. In discretion, as in prudence, of which it is a highly-developed form or perhaps quite simply a special name, the lights of reason and of faith come into focus, revealing what God is and what we are, the vital forces of humility and charity which are produced in our hearts as the proper result of these very efficacious lights. It is easy to understand, under these conditions, the role St. Catherine attributes to discretion and that she should entrust to it the whole conduct of our spiritual life. In her esteem, it is the immediate, interior, personal rule of that life; as such we shall now examine it.

⇧

The elaborations of the subject which we are about to quote will teach us nothing essentially new. They simply illustrate and render concrete what has preceded, entering into detail concerning some of the principal directions which discretion imposes upon our sentiments and actions. This is, besides, all that we need so as to be very clear about the role it plays and ought to play in our life, about the function it fulfills therein.

> But let us see, dearest daughter (now we will speak in particular, and so we shall be speaking in general too), what rule that virtue of discretion imposes on the soul. That rule seems to me to apply both to the soul and body of people who wish to live spiritually, in deed and thought. To be sure, it regulates every person in his rank and place: but let us now talk to ourselves. The first rule it gives to the soul is that we have mentioned--to render honor to God, goodwill to one's neighbor, and to oneself, hatred of sin and of one's own fleshliness. It regulates this charity toward the neighbor; for it is not willing to sacrifice the soul to him, since, in order to do him good or pleasure, it is not willing to offend God; but it flees from guilt discreetly, yet holds its body ready for every pain and torment, even to death, to rescue a soul, and as many souls as it can, from the hands of the devil. Also, it is ready to give up all its temporal possessions to help and rescue the body of its neighbor. Charity does this, when enlightened with discretion; for discretion should regulate one's charity to one's neighbor... And when measure and rule have been found in regard to

charity to the neighbor, discretion regulates also the matter which keeps the soul in that charity, and makes it grow--that is, in faithful, humble, and continual prayer; robing the soul in the cloak of desire for virtue, that it may not be injured by lukewarmness, negligence, or self-love, spiritual or temporal: therefore it inspires the soul with this desire for virtue, that its desire may not be placed on anything by which it might be deceived. Also, it rules and orders the creature physically, in this way: the soul which is prepared to wish for God makes its beginning as we have said; but because it has the vessel of its body, enlightened discretion must impose a rule on this, as it has done upon the soul, since the body ought to be a means for the increase of virtue. The rule withdraws it from the indulgences and luxuries of the world, and the conversation of worldlings; gives it conversation with the servants of God; takes it from dissolute places, and keeps it in places that stimulate devotion. It imposes restraint on all the members of the body, that they be modest and temperate: let the eye not look where it should not, but hold before itself earth, and heaven; let the tongue flee idle and vain speech, and be disciplined to proclaim the word of God for the salvation of the neighbor, and to confess its sins: let the ear flee agreeable, flattering, dissolute words, and any words of detraction that might be said to it; and let it hearken for the word of God, and the need of the neighbor, willingly listening to his necessity. So let the hand be swift in touching and working, and the feet in going: to all, discretion gives a rule. And that the perverse law of the flesh that fights against the spirit may not throw these tools into disorder, it imposes a rule upon the body, mortifying it with vigil, fast, and the other exercises which are all meant to bridle our body. But note, that all this is done, not indiscreetly, but with enlightened discretion. How is this shown? In this: that the soul does not place its chief desire in any act of penance. That it may not fall into such a fault as to take penance for its chief desire, enlightened discretion takes pains to robe the soul in the desire for virtue. Penance to be sure must be used as a tool, in due times and places, as need may be. If the flesh, being too strong, kicks against the spirit, penance takes the rod of discipline, and fast, and the cilice of many buds, and mighty vigils; and places burdens enough on the flesh, that it may be more subdued. But if the body is weak, fallen into illness, the rule of discretion does not approve of such a method. Nay, not only should fasting be abandoned, but flesh be eaten; if once a day is not enough, then four times. If one cannot stand up, let him stay on his bed; if he cannot kneel, let him sit or lie down, as he needs. This discretion demands. Therefore it insists that penance be treated as a means and not as a chief desire.[50]

And St. Catherine adds these words which I single out for special notice, for they are a protest against all spiritual materialism:

Do you not know why it must not be chief? That the soul may not serve God with a thing that can be taken from it and that is finite: but with holy desire, which is infinite, through its union with the infinite desire of God; and with the virtues which neither devil nor fellow-creature nor weakness can take from us, unless we choose. Herein must we make our foundation, and not in penance. No, in weakness the virtue of patience may be tested; in vexing conflicts with devils, fortitude and long perseverance; and in adversities suffered from our fellow-beings, humility, patience, and charity. So as to all other virtues--God lets them be tested by many contraries, but never taken from us, unless we choose. Herein must we make our foundation, and not in penance.

In all of this St. Catherine speaks from experience. She herself had had need of hearing from her divine Master the opportune lesson she here teaches to Daniella; she sets down in her *Dialogue* the heavenly instruction on the subject.[51] It must be acknowledged that her misunderstanding was of short duration and that she made no difficulty of allowing herself to be convinced. One senses in the advice she gives to Daniella all the strength of a firm conviction and of an experience which leaves no room for further hesitation.

Such, according to St. Catherine, is the role of discretion in the spiritual life; such are the principal directions it impresses upon that life.

---

[50] Letter T213; Scudder, pp. 146-148.

[51] *Dialogue*, chapter 11.

None of our actions escapes its control. It leaves its mark upon all of them: "These fruits... are all flavored with discretion."[52]

Filled with such thoughts, St. Catherine allows the spiritual enthusiasm welling up in her soul to overflow, that very characteristic enthusiasm which always pours forth from her as the result of an intellectual conviction clearly motivated and carefully analyzed, a well-defined, verified, reasoned perception of divine things.

> Holy discretion [is] that light which dissipates all darkness, takes away ignorance, and is the condiment of every instrument of virtue. Holy discretion is a prudence which cannot be cheated, a fortitude which cannot be beaten, a perseverance from end to end, stretching from heaven to earth, that is, from knowledge of Me to knowledge of self, and from love of Me to love of others. And the soul escapes dangers by her true humility, and, by her prudence, flies all the nets of the world and its creatures, and, with unarmed hands, that is through much endurance, discomfits the devil and the flesh with this sweet and glorious light; knowing, by it, her own fragility, she renders to her weakness its due of hatred.[53]

⇑

I wrote at the beginning of this study that in drawing the picture of discretion St. Catherine, without being aware of the fact, has given us a very striking self-portrait. Discretion is perhaps the distinctive trait of her spiritual physiognomy. Her exterior life bears the very profound and clearly-outlined seal of it. I am thinking particularly of that rare combination of boldness in her plans and imperturbable assurance in their execution whereby she reveals a soul conscious of what it is about and why. There is no trace of uncertainty as to the end in view nor hesitation regarding the practicality of the means selected. She gives the impression of a conscience sure of itself, with a prudence that grasps firmly all the threads of her actions. No doubt a special light of divine origin enlightens her; but she manifestly appropriates it, incorporates it in herself, fixes upon it by stable, vital interior virtues so that, under these miraculous illuminations, it is truly she herself who undertakes the

---

[52] *Dialogue*, chapter 10.

[53] *Dialogue*, chapter 11.

conduct of her life. Yes, it is she and not her directors of conscience, however much she may hold them in esteem and submit to them wholeheartedly. In reality, few women saints have been less directed than St. Catherine.

One of the most revealing incidents from this point of view is the touching story of St. Catherine's ministry toward Niccolò di Tuldo, the young conspirator of Perugia. Her design was audacious; it would be naïve to deny it. Evidently even she was aware of the fact. But observe her in the fulfillment of her delicate mission which was still further complicated by the somewhat indiscreet requests of Tuldo. There is not a trace of hesitation or uncertainty, but the supreme assurance of a soul completely resolved both as to the object and as to the means. The virtue of discretion—which, for Catherine, is in no sense a negative virtue, advising abstention, blindly counseling reserve or what timid, pusillanimous souls are wont to style safest and most prudent—the virtue of discretion is displayed there magnificently . But from beginning to the end of St. Catherine's life, the same thing is true.

VI. Patience

Among other traits, St. Catherine has this in common with St. Thomas Aquinas, that she perceives the real conditions of human life with as much competence and penetration as she does the highest mysteries of divine life and evaluates them with a very reliable judgment. She is far removed from any taint of the chimerical. St. Teresa of Avila herself, so admirable from this point of view, is not however endowed with any more good sense and practical foresight.

Not only is she well aware of our common misery, but she shares it; especially have the trials of all kinds, in the midst of which our life is painfully unfolded, also surrounded her own. It seems to me impossible not to be struck by this when one studies the teaching of St. Catherine regarding patience. She reveals herself therein, to a truly touching degree, as belonging to our race, as one of us, our sister in humanity and, in every wise, the counselor of whom we have need.

⇧

What St. Catherine singles out first of all concerning patience is the close bond uniting it to charity. "Consider," God the Father tells her, "that the love of divine charity is so closely joined in the soul with perfect patience, that neither can leave the soul without the other."[54] Therefore, in her mind, patience is the most certain mark of the presence of charity in a soul. It is "patience which proves that I am in the soul and the soul in Me.... Patience...is...a demonstrative sign, whether a soul be in a state of grace and truly loves or not."[55] Patience, if I may dare to say so, is the humble, gentle face of charity.

Then Catherine qualifies her thought by an explanation. It is from charity that patience flows. She received the categorical declaration of the sovereign Master on this point.

> Since they love Me for Myself, because I am the supreme Goodness and worthy of being loved; since they love themselves for My sake and their neighbors for Me, that is to say, so as to render praise and glory to My name, on that account they are patient, enduring with courage and perseverance.[56]

Let no one be deceived. Patience does not proceed from charity in the same way as the other supernatural virtues. It is not merely one of numerous fruits, a haphazard effect of love; it is its natural effect, primary, essential and characteristic. "For this reason (if the soul elects to love Me) she should elect to endure pains for Me in whatever mode or circumstance I may send them to her."[57] This amounts to saying that charity is extended, developed and completed by patience. Nor do these formulae yet exhaust the concept formed by Catherine. She has a very expressive remark on the subject of the relations between patience and love, a remark pregnant with shrewd psychology and life experience, which she repeats constantly, interpreting as it does one of the master

---

[54] *Dialogue*, chapter 5.

[55] *Dialogue*, chapters 10 and 154.

[56] *Dialogue*, chapter 76.

[57] *Dialogue*, chapter 5.

thoughts of her spiritual doctrine: "Patience is the marrow of charity."[58] Catherine dares to go even so far. She who has so carefully analyzed charity, describing it as a love, a supernatural affection of our hearts for God, now declares it to be a form of patience. That is certainly what she means. Here on earth patience is an essential element of charity, that which characterizes it, supports it and gives it consistency. What, then, is her conception of patience?

In the terminology of St. Catherine the word "patience" has a synonym which is "endurance." She writes: "Patience endures injuries, small or grant, wherever they may come. It endures all with a peaceful, tranquil soul."[59] And elsewhere: "Who, then, would not be drawn to love this sweet virtue of patience, that is to say, of endurance for the sake of Christ crucified?"[60]

Patience is therefore primarily an endurance. But of what? St. Catherine makes use of a term at once simple and profound, such as only life's experiences could have suggested, to describe the object of this endurance. It is the function of patience to endure fatigue. According to Catherine, *fatigue* is the word which best expresses what we often call, borrowing a term from the Gospels, the burden of life. She means by that the heaped up load of various trials which compose all of our lives. It is their repercussion in the very depths of our soul. How well we can sense that Catherine had experienced this fatigue, with all her value and courage! She so often enumerates its diverse elements, with a kind of melancholy satisfaction: fatigue of body and of soul, the fatigue of exhausting tasks, of powerless efforts, of human injustice, of separations and divisions, of interior struggles and trials. All of this fatigue must be borne manfully, with a calm and gentle spirit. That is the object of patience.

But is that the whole of patience? No; St. Catherine adds to this analysis certain other elements. She writes to her noble hostess in Genoa, Madonna Orietta Scotta:

---

[58] *Dialogue*, chapters 10, 95, 154, etc.

[59] Letter to the King of Hungary, Louis of Anjou; T357.

[60] Letter to Friar Raymond of Capua; T104.

This virtue [of patience] shows the light by which the patient soul is enlighted. It shows that the soul, by the light of holy faith, has seen and recognized that God desires nothing but her good and that whatever He bestows and permits in this life He does so for our sanctification. That is why the soul who has realized this truth by that very fact becomes patient. When her sensual passions try to raise their heads and manifest themselves by impatience, she says to herself: "So you want to grieve at your own well-being? You cannot, nor should you grieve but endure without any dissimulation for the glory and praise of God's name."[61]

Patience is therefore not merely bearing with the fatigues and burdens of this life. Even an animal, a poor beast that toils and suffers, is patient in that sense. Our patience ought to be based upon our conviction, on the one hand, that God wills our good and, on the other, that nothing happens to us without His order or permission. It is a conscious, enlightened, motivated, truly human and supernatural endurance.

Finally, patience is endurance out of love for God and for His Christ, loving endurance; and this last trait brings us back to the beginning of our study, completing its explanation and justification. In a letter to Monna Giovanna Pazzi, St. Catherine writes:

Now, I wish you to know, dear daughter of mine, that what God does or permits in this life is done to insure our salvation or increase our perfection. We ought, therefore, humbly and patiently to accept it with respect; we shall do this if we open the eyes of our intellect to consider with what charity and intensity of love and not hatred, we shall receive it in love.[62]

Patience, then, is endurance, enlightened, reasonably motivated and inspired by love. In patience charity becomes strengthened by enduring for the sake of the God she loves the trials He sends her through love. Lastly, when St. Catherine writes: "In this sweet and holy garment of patience does the soul clothe herself when she puts on the will of God," what does she mean but that patience consists in the loving conformity

---

[61] Letter T355.

[62] Letter T87.

of our will with God's? And is not this very conformity one of the essential elements of charity? The words quoted at the beginning, then: "Patience is the marrow of charity," should, it seems to me, no longer surprise us.

⇧

St. Catherine is never weary of exhorting her disciples and correspondents to patience. She recommends its practice to them and encourages them thereto by various considerations which may be grouped under two headings: the necessity for patience and its benefits.

As for the necessity of practicing patience, Catherine seems to be extraordinarily convinced of it. She affirms and explains its need constantly in all her letters. For instance, she writes to the Florentine, Niccolò Soderini:

> Very dear father in the sweet Christ Jesus, I Catherine, servant and slave of the servants of Jesus Christ, write you in His precious blood with the desire of seeing you established in a true and holy patience. In fact, without patience, we should not be pleasing to God and could not persevere in the state of grace.

A little further on in the same letter she clarifies and completes her thought. Patience "is that virtue which never sets itself in disagreement with the will of God."[63] Its function is to maintain harmony between our will and God's. In a way, it becomes identified with this necessary harmony without which it is undoubtedly impossible to persevere in the friendship of God. As can be seen, it concerns the primary interests of our spiritual life.

But why can there be no persevering conformity between our will and God's without patience? Catherine will tell us. She writes to Monna Nella, widow of a certain Buonconti of Pisa:

> Oh dearest mother, among all the virtues patience is the most necessary. For we do not pass through the ocean of life without being lashed by countless tribulations. Wherever we turn our ship, this ocean beats us with its waves. The demon adds his temptations. What he cannot do by himself, he does through

---

[63] Letter T297.

the medium of creatures. He settles himself in the heart and on the tongue of his servants. Moreover he clouds the vision of the intellect causing it to see what does not exist. Then our heart is filled with diverse thoughts, with bitterness toward our neighbor and often toward the one who loves us most.

This results in words that wound, in ill-natured behavior, misunderstandings, impatience, hatred and rancor. "And thus," she concludes, "we deprive ourselves of the life of love."[64] It is here that patience intervenes, the sovereign efficacy of which St. Catherine extols in the following terms:

> Oh true and gentle patience, you are that virtue which is never vanquished, but always triumphant... You dissolve hatred of heart and its rancor. You dispel bitterness against one's neighbor. You comfort the soul in all its griefs. Thanks to you, the heavy burdens of countless tribulations become light. Thanks to you, disgust is transformed into sweetness.[65]

Thus, one of the most redoubtable dangers menacing the conformity of our will with God's is tribulation under its many forms, external and internal. The frail craft, tossed about exceedingly, threatens to break adrift and be carried far from God amid the briny ocean spray. It is patience which steadies and saves it.

Patience is no less beneficial than it is necessary. St. Catherine treats of it and extols it as the source of the most precious advantages the soul can enjoy here below. The first fruit of patience is self-possession, equanimity. She writes to Monna Lodovica di Granello: "Having become patient, the soul is neither scandalized nor disturbed by anything."[66] To Madonna Orietta Scotta she says: "Patience is strong, dispelling impatience and anxiety."[67] And to Niccolò Soderini: "She is a queen dominating impatience and not allowing herself to be vanquished by anger."[68] Finally, in the same letter, we read this fine sentence so well

---

[64] Letter T151.

[65] Ibid.

[66] Letter T304.

[67] Letter T355.

[68] Letter T297.

depicting the serene peace wherein the patient soul abides: "With this sweet and glorious virtue, on the stormy sea of countless fatigues, man takes his rest."[69]

Patience does more than merely establish us in peace. It keeps us active, enterprising in well-doing. This is another of its benefits and an incalculable one. Trials upset and weary the impatient soul. They have no hold upon the patient man, neither upon his courage nor upon his vitality. "The patient soul," Catherine writes to Niccolò Soderini, "never regrets the good she has done whence she often draws fatigue and tribulation."[70] To Madonna Orietta Scotta she says: "It is never deterred by any fatigue, for it is united to charity...It is endowed with long-suffering perseverance. No matter what fatigue presents itself, it never looks back but ever advances, following the humble Lamb whose patience and meekness were so great that never did He raise His voice in complaint."[71]

Finally, patience is a fountain pouring forth joy. "Patience," she writes to Madonna Orietta Scotta, "causes a sweetness to well up in the center of the heart."[72] To Messer Francesco da Montalcino she explains its cause:

> Beloved brother in the sweet Christ Jesus, I Catherine, servant and slave of the servants of Jesus Christ, write to you in His precious blood with the desire of seeing you established in a true and holy patience, considering that without patience we cannot please God but would taste the first fruits of hell. How foolish would that man be who would wish to taste of hell when he might enjoy eternal life! If I look at it correctly, eternal life consists in nothing but a will peacefully conformed and submissive to the sweet will of God, in such wise that we can only desire or will what God wills. And all the joy possessed by those who really rejoice is founded upon this peaceful will.[73]

---

[69] Ibid.

[70] Ibid.

[71] Letter T355.

[72] Ibid.

[73] Letter T5.

But this will peacefully conformed to God's will is in us the effect of patience and, in fact, patience itself. It is therefore quite true that patience is in us the source of eternal joy.

Then St. Catherine, profoundly stirred by this conviction of the necessity for patience, full of gratitude for the experience each day brought to her of its benefits, proceeds to pour out her soul in the following hymn of praise, somewhat subtle in expression but nevertheless very touching and noble in sentiment:

> O patience, how lovable you are! O patience, what hope you bestow on him who possess you! O patience, you are a queen ruling over anger and never ruled by her! O patience, you work justice even upon sensuality when it would lifts its head in wrath. You grasp in hand the two-edged sword which cuts down and extirpates anger, pride and that marrow of pride which is impatience! Those two edges are hatred and love. You are clothed in a garment of sun, garbed as you are in the light of true knowledge of God and the ardor of divine charity. You dart forth rays which strike those who do you harm; you heap burning coals of charity upon their heads. The hatred of their hearts is burned and consumed therein. Yes, sweet patience founded on charity, you bear fruit in one's neighbor and render honor to God. Your robe is strewn with the stars of the various virtues. In fact, patience is not to be found in the soul without the stars of all the virtues. Self-knowledge precedes it as the light of the moon whereby the night is illumined. Then comes the day, the brilliance and ardor with which patience is clothed as with the sun. Who, then, would not be enamored of this sweet thing which is patience.[74]

⚜

It seems to me, having reached the end of this study, that St. Catherine would urge us affectionately to exercise ourselves in patience. I can hear her addressing to us this prayer which she formerly made to her brother, Benincasa, when the latter, wincing under the tactics of their mother, Lapa, became angry and gave vent to recriminations:

---

[74] Letter to Friar Raymond of Capua; T104.

So I beg you, in order that you may receive the fruit of your tribulations, that you assume the armor of patience. And should it seem very hard to you to endure your many troubles, bear in memory three things, that you may endure more patiently. First, I want you to think of the shortness of your time, for on one day you are not certain of the morrow. We may truly say that we do not feel past trouble, nor that which is to come, but only the moment of time at which we are. Surely, then, we ought to endure patiently, since the time is so short. The second thing is, for you to consider the fruit which follows our troubles. For St. Paul says there is no comparison between our troubles and the fruit and reward of supernal glory. The third is, for you to consider the loss which results to those who endure in wrath and impatience; for loss follows this here, and eternal punishment to the soul. Therefore I beg you, dearest brother, to endure in all patience.[75]

VII. Fortitude

Both in her *Dialogue* and in her letters, St. Catherine frequently extols the supernatural virtue of fortitude. From the way in which she speaks of it, one can easily see that she considers fortitude, especially when combined with that patience and "long perseverance" with which she is pleased to associate it, as one of the principal resources of our Christian life. The pages she devotes to it abound, as usual, in keen observations dictated by her experience of life and in wonderfully profound intuitions. If one can distinctly perceive therein the vigorous, amply-timed pulsations of that spiritual intensity, that burning love wherewith Catherine's soul was consumed, no idle sensibility or vain imagination is to be found. Everything about it is sound and solid; all of it is true charity and pure light; all is divine life.

Nevertheless, I admit that, to coordinate St. Catherine's statements on the virtue of fortitude, bring them into prominence and formulate a consistent, if not systematic, teaching on the subject, requires some application. In all humility and without departing from the reverence and love outside of which her thought would remain obscure and remote

---

[75] Letter T18; Scudder, p. 30.

from us, let us try to group her assertions under the following headings: the *necessity*, the *source* and the *effects* of the virtue of fortitude.

⇑

There is no need of lengthy reasoning to establish the fact that without the supernatural virtue of fortitude the Christian life is impossible. St. Catherine takes experience as her starting point:

> Very dear son in Christ Jesus, I, Catherine...write to you in His precious blood, with the desire of seeing you strong and persevering in the struggle, that you may receive the crown of glory.... But you will say to me: "How can I attain such fortitude, for I am weak to such a point that a mere nothing suffices to throw me down."

It is a well beloved disciple, Stefano Maconi, who is supposed to be presenting this objection and, without the least demur, St. Catherine acknowledges that it is a sound one: "I answer," she goes on, "by recognizing that you are indeed weak and frail insofar as your sensuality is concerned."[76] Such is our native state: a weakness and frailty without limits residing in our "sensuality", with its source in "the sensual love of self." For it is quite evident that the situation described above is not confined to Stefano Maconi. St. Catherine explains to another of her disciples, San di Maco, that in this regard we are all in the same condition and, however platitudinous they may appear at first glance, the observations with which this state inspires her, are by no means unprofitable. We are so inclined to lose sight, either in the direction of presumption or—which is no improvement—in that of discouragement or fear, to lose sight of this fact of experience and common sense. "If you tell me," she writes therefore to Sano, If you tell me, very dear son: 'I am weak against so many enemies,' I will answer and admit that, of ourselves, we are indeed all weak and frail so as to fall on account of a mere nothing."[77]

On the other hand, feeble, hesitant creatures that we are, we find ourselves thrown into the midst of the fray, into the chaotic battle of life, amid countless enemies whose furious assaults or treacherous surprise

---

[76] Letter T195.

[77] Letter T142.

attacks we have reason to fear from moment to moment, on every side at once, from within no less than from without. St. Catherine knows this better than anyone and repeats it unceasingly. Thus she writes to Friar Matteo Tolomei and to Dom Nicolò di Francia, both of them religious, for all that: "We cannot withdraw from the struggle for as long as we inhabit this mortal body, whatever be the condition under which we live. Each one must sustain it insofar as it pleases the goodness of God to send it to him."[78]

Against these enemies, against their incessant and divisive attacks, our duty is to face the issue watchfully and courageously. To the two correspondents just mentioned, St. Catherine expressly declares:

> Most dear sons in the sweet Christ Jesus, I, Catherine...write you in His precious blood with the desire of seeing you struggle earnestly on this field of battle. Never on any account should you look backwards. Like a brave knight devoid of all base fear, remain firm in the midst of the blows.[79]

Considering what we are, it is quite evident that, given such a situation and such an assignment, we are lost beforehand unless a divine strength takes possession of our weakness, coursing through us so as to transform us completely. It would be childish to ask this strength in external supports. Nevertheless, that is a common, tenacious illusion: "To this power of true and real virtues," Catherine observes to Cardinal Bonaventura of Padua, "neither wealth nor exterior position, nor worldly honors nor high offices nor self-assurance lead us."[80] Our weakness lies within ourselves. That is where Christian fortitude should appear.

⚜

But whence shall we draw this fortitude; what is its source? In the letter to Stefano Maconi already quoted St. Catherine expresses herself in these terms: "You are feeble and weak with respect to sensuality; but with respect to reason and strength of mind it is altogether otherwise, since we are made steadfast in the blood of Christ. It is in sensuality

---

[78] Letter T169.

[79] Ibid.

[80] Letter T334.

alone that our weakness resides."[81] In the reason, the "mind", the higher, spiritual part of our being, then, is to be found, if not the primary source, at lease the original, principal seat of that fortitude with which God has endowed us. Our will in particular is an impregnable fortress so long as it does not itself surrender. St. Catherine is pleased to repeat this often to her correspondents. She writes to Pietro Marquis del Monte:

> Very dear son, we see that God has provided man with so powerful a weapon that neither devil nor any creature can harm him; and this weapon is the free will of man.... God intends that we should make use of the weapon He has given us, that by its means we may parry the blows we receive from our enemies.... If a man does not divest himself of this arm, if he does not yield himself into the hands of the demon by giving his consent, he is never overcome.[82]

However, this is not yet the supernatural virtue of fortitude, but only its beginning. Such fortitude, centered in our reason and our will, ought to be exercised, to subject all the rebellious elements of our nature to itself, to radiate upon even our sensitive powers, establishing itself under the form of a living, stable discipline in the very heart of that sensuality wherein our weakness dwells. That is a laborious, difficult undertaking. Let us hear St. Catherine describing for us its general development:

> I therefore wish, my beloved children, that in all things you apply yourself to destroying this perverse sensitive will which ceaselessly desires to rebel against God. Behold the manner of setting about it. Sit upon the elevated throne of your conscience so as to judge yourself. Do not let the slightest thought to which God does not assent to pass without a stern correction. A man ought to separate himself into two parts, sensibility and reason. Reason ought to draw from the scabbard the two-edged sword of hatred for vice and love of virtue. Armed with this sword, it compels sensuality to sue for mercy. It uproots and tears out of the soul every manner of vice and of disorderly impulse. Never

---

[81] Letter T195.

[82] Letter T148.

does it indulge this slave in any of its desires; but with love of virtue it tramples them under the feet of the will.[83]

In this wise the supremacy of reason and will over sensuality is stabilized. Thus the virtue of fortitude, emanating from our reason and our will, establishes itself in the very heart of our sensibility so as to subject the latter to our spiritual nature, to moderate and regulate that whole world of vain fears and foolhardy indiscretions both of which are inimical to real fortitude. Once again, the undertaking is hazardous; one may well ask if our reason and our will shall accomplish their end. St. Catherine has no doubt about it. But she considers it necessary above all to strengthen and increase even the fortitude of our reason and will so as to insure to them all the possible power of acting, rendering them efficacious in their domination. This is, no doubt, primarily the role of divine grace, as she is careful not to forget. She writes to Pietro Marquis del Monte: "The weapon is trusty and excellent is our auxiliary, namely God, who no one can resist."[84] But she declares that our own part remains a large one in the development of Christian fortitude and, repeatedly, she undertakes to analyze this part and the means of accomplishing it. We now enter upon an entirely practical sphere; we are at the very wellsprings of the virtue of fortitude insofar as they are present within us. She writes to Cardinal Bonaventura of Padua:

That is why the soul who abides in that sweet cell of the knowledge of self and of God's goodness humbles herself interiorly. For that which is not can hardly take pride in itself. Now she sees, as has been said, that she does not exist by herself but by God.... Hence the ardor of charity grows within her because she recognizes that she depends upon God for her very being and all the gifts that are added thereto. Since she perceives that the unworthy law of sin, ever fighting against the spirit, brings about the loss of God and of the fruit of the Blood, if the will consents to it, she therefore immediately conceives a holy hatred for her own sensuality; and the more she detests it the more she loves reason. With this love and this light she

---

[83] Letter to Francesco di Pipino, a tailor of Florence, and to Monna Agnesa, his wife; T265.

[84] Letter T148.

withdraws from that which rendered her weak and by the affection of love is united to God, the sovereign Fortitude, by the bond of true, real virtues.[85]

This two-edged sword—hatred for vice and love of virtue—of which reason has need so as to compel sensuality to sue for mercy, is the knowledge of self and of God who insures its possession to her.

Elsewhere, to arrive at the same goal, St. Catherine opens up to us a somewhat different pathway, or perhaps the same one considered under a new light. We read in the letter to Stefano Maconi already quoted:

I say that it is in the following manner we may acquire the glorious virtue of fortitude and enduring perseverance. When reason has been confirmed in the blood of Christ, we ought to renounce ourselves in this sweet and glorious treasure. With the eye of the intellect and the light of holy faith we discover it in the vessel of our soul; we realize that our being comes from God; we see that God has restored us to the life of grace in the blood of His only Son and that thus our weakness has vanished. O beloved son, behold and rejoice that you have become a vessel containing the blood of Christ crucified, provided only that you consent to taste it by the affection of love.... O Blood...you inflame and consume the soul in the fire of divine charity; that is to say, you consume all that is to be found in the soul contrary to the will of God.... O most sweet Blood, you rid her of sensual self-love which weakens the soul who is wrapped in it and you enfold her in the flames of divine charity; for she cannot taste you, O Blood, without being enveloped and clothed by you in flames: You were indeed poured forth by the ardor of love.... That is why love is not to be found without fortitude, nor fortitude without perseverance; that is why, moreover, it fortifies and strengthens in all adversity. Behold then, most sweet son, such is the way to attain perfect fortitude, namely: unite yourself to the fire of divine charity which you will find in the Blood and which, in this Blood, quenches all self-will, causing it to die. Then, leaning upon the sovereign Fortitude, you will be strong and persevering and will cause the

---

[85] Letter T334.

weakness of your own sensuality to disappear. In bitterness you will taste sweetness and in the midst of war, peace.[86]

This knowledge of self and of God, which St. Catherine has already told us is the means of acquiring the virtue of fortitude, she here renders more precise insofar as it should have as its principal object the mystery of Jesus, His blood poured out for us and filling our souls, the love of which this blood-shedding is a pledge and symbol. The knowledge of self and of God has as its effect, according to the thought of Catherine, the enkindling in our minds of a clear, inextinguishable light, in our wills a burning love, and thereby heightening to the extreme limit their fortitude, their power to act and to govern. All of this work finally results in substituting one love for another in our wills, the love of God for the ill-regulated love of self. It is this love, this divine charity, which is our fortitude. Thanks to it our free-will is capable of maintaining the difficult role our saint ascribed to it earlier, that of imposing its sovereign law upon our sense faculties, bringing them into subjection, rendering them pliable to its action, enabling them to share even in its strength.

⇧

St. Catherine is now about to describe to us the effects of the virtue of fortitude in the soul possessed of it. It is here above all that she speaks from experience. One recognizes this from the fervor of her words. She writes to Cardinal Bonaventura of Padua:

> It is therefore very true that in this self-knowledge of which we have spoken the soul acquires fortitude. To what extent does she become strong, very dear father? To the point where neither demons nor creatures can cause her to waver so long as she remains united to her strength and nothing can separate her from that strength against her will. Can the battles and persecutions of the world make this soul falter? Assuredly not. Rather does she draw greater fortitude from them, for she finds in them opportunities of taking refuge with still greater earnestness in her strength. In this wise, moreover, the love she has for God is able to test itself and discover whether it is a mercenary love or not, whether it tends toward its own

---

[86] Letter T195.

satisfaction. Creatures cannot cause her to weaken by their constantly renewed persecutions, their injustices, outrages, reproaches, contempt and insults. On the contrary, they cause her to withdraw ever more and more from all love of creatures outside of the Creator and to exercise herself in the virtue of patience. There is therefore nothing that can make the soul falter, unless a man consents thereto by separating himself from his strength. This is true, no matter in what situation a man may find himself, for neither any situation nor any combination of circumstances can take God from us. God considers neither condition nor place nor time. He is concerned only with holy and sincere desire.[87]

Thus, far from harming a soul strengthened by the virtue of fortitude, struggles and difficulties only procure for her the opportunity of drawing closer her union with God who is her strength, proving her love for Him and establishing herself in patience. Such are the benefits of fortitude.

St. Catherine does not contemplate them without being moved. She perceives so clearly that the path to which fortitude commits us while providing us with courage to persevere therein is not only the way of salvation but furthermore the way enabling us to advance without excessive suffering, in serenity and peace among the conflicts of life. She exclaims in the *Dialogue*:

Oh how happy is that soul who, while still in this mortal body already enjoys an immortal good! She holds all things in reverence [What a beautiful word and how exquisite a sentiment!]. She is as satisfied with the right hand as with the left, with tribulation as with consolation, with hunger and thirst as with food and drink, with cold as with heat, with nakedness as with clothing, with life as with death, with praise as with blame, with affliction as with comfort. In all things she remains firm and steadfast because the living rock is her foundation. By the light of faith and enduring hope, she has seen and acknowledged that I can give all with the same love and the same object, which is your salvation, and that I provide for everything. That is why in great labors I give proportionate

---

[87] Letter T334.

strength, nor do I place any burden upon your shoulders except what they can bear, provided you dispose yourself with willingness to bear it for love of Me.[88]

What can I add to such sublime and convincing words? This ideal of Christian fortitude is worthy of captivating our souls. If we do not dare flatter ourselves that we accomplish it perfectly, at least nothing forbids us and everything urges us to tend toward it in the footsteps of St. Catherine.

Second Part

VIII. Faith

Whatever the subject of which she speaks, St. Catherine does so with intense fervor of expression and of conception. This does not facilitate the task of discovering which spiritual values she places in the foreground. Yet this must be done if we would truly understand her teaching in its most characteristic features.

Nevertheless, it is impossible not to be struck by the materially very considerable place occupied by the virtue of faith in her writings. By merely skimming through them one receives a vivid impression that she must have for it a particular esteem, a privileged devotion. This should not surprise us. Is she not the daughter of the Patriarch Dominic and sister to St. Peter Martyr and St. Thomas Aquinas?

Let us gather up reverently then her scattered observations on this great subject; not all of them, for they are too numerous, but the most significant ones. In order to understand them better, let us attempt to set them in order, deliberately, quietly, by a humble effort, after the fashion of a schoolboy. Do not smile at us, Catherine. You are so keen and our minds are plodding. Help us rather, if you will!

"It is necessary for him who is lifted with desire to learn the Truth with the light of faith;" and a little further on: "With the light of a lively faith, she opened the eye of her intellect upon the Eternal Truth." These formulae which recur on every page of St. Catherine's writings are

---

[88] *Dialogue*, chapter 141.

remarkably accurate and very expressive in their simplicity. The intellect is the eye of our soul. Like that of the body, it has its pupil which is the virtue of faith which must be understood as an interior and permanent light. The object of this light or pupil is Truth, "the sweet, Supreme and First Truth."[89]

Is the virtue of faith, then, the characteristic natural light of our intellect? No, it is a supernatural light of grace.

> Man knows all these things only by means of the light wherewith You enlighten the intellect which is, among the powers of the soul, the most noble. It is the light of faith which You bestow upon every Christian when, in the sacrament of baptism, You pour into him the light of faith and of grace whereby You purify him from the original sin which he had contracted. Indeed, You have given us a light capable of leading us to the last end of Beatitude.[90]

This light or pupil of faith, received from God in baptism together with sanctifying grace, is therefore of the supernatural, divine order by its quality as well as by its origin. Hence it is a light upon the very God of our eternal Beatitude. All of this is the most solid and accurate theology.

St. Catherine insists on the absolute need for this light of faith.

> The knowledge of My Truth, which knowledge, the intellect (which is the eye of the soul) illuminated in Me, possesses. This eye has the pupil of the most holy faith, which light of faith enables the soul to discern, to know, and to follow the way and the doctrine of My Truth—the Word Incarnate; and without this pupil of faith she would not see, except as a man who has the form of the eye, but who has covered the pupil (which causes the eye to see) with a cloth. So the pupil of the intellect is faith, and if the soul has covered it with the cloth of infidelity,

---

[89] *Dialogue*, chapter 87.

[90] Prayer of St. Catherine of Siena. Cartier edition of the *Dialogue*, prayer 13; Art Catholique edition (1919), prayer 13; Bernard edition (*Vie Spirituelle*, 123), p. 27.

drawn over it by self-love, she does not see, but only has the form of the eye without the light, because she has hidden it.[91]

These words invite us to examine in more detail how St. Catherine conceives of the relations between the intellect and faith, natural light and supernatural light. Her observations on this subject are deserving of attentive consideration. Sometimes the terms she uses are rather difficult to define precisely.

We read in chapter 98 of the *Dialogue*: "You know...that, without the light, no one can walk in the truth, that is, without the light of reason, which light of reason you draw from Me, the True Light, by means of the eye of your intellect and the light of faith which I have given you in holy baptism." The reason here referred to is therefore not natural reason, but Christian reason, that is, reason enlightened by faith.

> For, in baptism, and through the mediation of the Blood of My only begotten Son, you have received the form of faith [in other words, the virtue of faith]; which faith you exercise in virtue by the [proper, natural] light of reason, which gives you life and causes you to walk in the path of truth, and, by its means, to arrive at Me, the True Light, for, without it, you would plunge into darkness.[92]

Reason has therefore its light as the virtue of faith has its own, and these two lights are associated. The virtue of faith makes use of the light of reason in exercising itself. Reason, on the other hand, finds itself illumined by the supernatural light of faith which becomes its own to such a degree that Catherine finally attributes to reason (enlightened by faith) the privilege of guiding us in the way of Truth. This is remarkable teaching which St. Thomas Aquinas would not reject.

Regarding this close solidarity between reason and faith, St. Catherine goes even further in a letter to the Florentine lawyer, Ristoro Canigiani. If it happens that faith, in its struggle against sensuality, experiences rebuffs and is eclipsed by dangerous shadows, reason comes to its aid.

---

[91] *Dialogue*, chapter 45.

[92] *Dialogue*, chapter 98.

Very dear son in the sweet Christ Jesus, I, Catherine, the servant and slave of the servants of Jesus Christ, write you in His precious Blood with the desire of seeing you stir up the light [all the light, it would seem, of reason and faith] which God has given to you. It must grow in you unceasingly. For without perfect light we can neither know nor love Truth, nor clothe ourselves in it once again. Unless we do re-clothe ourselves therein, we shall end up by transforming our very light into darkness. Everyone ought therefore to possess it in its perfection, whatever be his state.

Up to this point all is clear in these observations which evince so marked a taste for light. But let us continue reading:

Wherein is its perfection revealed...? In the fact that it embraces with love the Truth it has known, that it is attracted to virtue while detesting vice and that selfish sensuality which is the source of all sins and an evil law constantly struggling against the spirit. It then shows that its vision is perfect and that the cloud of infidelity has not obscured the pupil of the mind's eye, that is, the light of most holy faith. For if our light were imperfect, we would see with a natural light (thenceforth but slightly or not at all illumined by the obscured light of faith). Nor should we otherwise put into practice what we knew, nor make use of that [natural] light with love for the virtues.

How are we to escape from this state if we happen to fall into it? Here we have touched upon the very point which elucidates the peculiar teaching of our text.

We ought therefore to apply ourselves to arousing this natural light [imperfect, that is, rather than purely natural or rational], so that this imperfection may be removed and we may come to perfect knowledge.... But how, very dear son, shall we succeed in reaching perfect light? I shall tell you: with the help of the light [ever the light!] and in the following manner. We have within us a natural light [in a new sense, this time, meaning the light proper to reason itself], which God has given to us [in creating us] to render us capable of distinguishing good from evil.... This is a discernment with which God has endowed our very nature.... With this first light, however imperfect it may be [if we make use of it to judge and repel the deceitful suggestions of sensuality], we shall acquire a perfect supernatural light [that of faith restored to its own brightness] which graces will shed upon our soul. This perfect light [according to the same formula applied at the beginning of this text] will attach us to virtue.... It will establish us in permanent agreement with the sweet will of God.... The first light [that of reason], if we arouse it, separates us [from transitory or harmful things]; the second attaches and unites us to virtue.[93]

Allied together, the lights of reason and of faith are opposed to sensuality, their common enemy. If it happens that, in this conflict, the light of faith is eclipsed and more or less overshadowed, the less perfect light of reason which nevertheless, since it belongs to nature itself, is more tenacious, ought to come to the aid of faith and so it does in effect.

How glorious is that light of most holy faith wherewith the soul has seen, known and still knows my Truth. She has received from the Lord, the Holy Spirit, this [perfect] light. It is a supernatural light which the soul receives from My Goodness by using her natural lights.[94]

Then St. Catherine goes so far as to pronounce those bold words wherein she affirms her conception, so precisely Thomistic, of faith and its vital relationship with reason: "Reason holds in itself the light of faith, and one is not lost without the other."[95] This is one of the places were we touch the solid rock upon which her spiritual teaching is built.

⇧

Like reason, the virtue of faith is closely allied to the will, that is, to the virtue of charity. In a hundred different connections St. Catherine reminds us of this. Over and over again she declares the action of charity upon faith and that of faith upon charity.

The action of charity upon faith is twofold, general and special. Its general action is only a particular instance of that which it exerts on all

---

[93] Letter T301.

[94] *Dialogue*, chapter 141.

[95] *Dialogue*, chapter 51.

the supernatural virtues. Since it constitutes their form, charity makes them perfect virtues or, to use a more concrete and perhaps more familiar term, "living" virtues. Let us listen to St. Catherine as she tells us what this action consists in with regard to faith. She writes, for example, to the prior of the Olivetan monks of Florence, Fra Jacopo: "From love is born living faith.... The virtues, not dead but living, have love for their mother, that is to say, divine charity."[96] This vitalizing action, as she recognizes, is exerted to the advantage of all the virtues, not of faith alone. Nevertheless, charity vivifies each of the supernatural virtues according to its own nature.

With regard to faith, St. Catherine abounds in detailed descriptions of the vitality or fruitfulness which it derives from charity. Since the theological virtue of faith is, in the scheme of knowledge of God and of ourselves in God, the generating virtue of our whole supernatural life, its action, animated by charity, extends to everything. All the other supernatural virtues, every form of spiritual good and progress, receive from it both direction and effective promotion. Since we cannot treat of the subject in its entirety, let us confine ourselves to what is most characteristic in this beneficent fecundity of living faith. We read, for example, in a letter to Monna Niera Gambacorta of Pisa, the aunt of our Blessed Clare Gambacorta:

> Know that it is love which makes of us [effective] believers. We have faith in what we love. Hence we see that the true servants of God, through the love they bear Him [and which animates their faith], lose all faith and hope in themselves.... As soon as one loves with faith [Catherine, why do you not rather say: as soon as one believes with love? Is that not your meaning?], living hope appears, no longer trusting in self, but in Him who is. Such as these have a faith that is living, not dead, with sweet and holy works.[97]

Still more explicitly St. Catherine writes to Monna Mitarella, wife of the Sienese senator, Vico da Mogliano:

> You have sent me word of the risk incurred by the Senator [on the occasion of a popular uprising], regarding which I see that

---

[96] Letter T32.

[97] Letter T224.

you experienced great fright, that you had neither faith nor hope in the prayers of God's servants. That is why I beg you, on the part of God and of Jesus, our most sweet Love, to persevere in this sweet and holy faith. O sweet faith which gives us life! If you abide in this holy faith, your heart shall never know sadness. For sadness has no other source than our faith in creatures. Creatures are dead, vain things which give way. But our heart can find repose only in firm, stable things. Man lives today, tomorrow he will be dead. Hence, if we wish to find repose, it is expedient for us by faith and love to take care to rest our heart upon Jesus crucified.[98]

But how does living faith secure for our souls the benefit of this firmness, stability and serenity? St. Catherine explains to us:

If tribulations on man's account, or infirmity, or poverty, or change of worldly condition, or loss of children, or of other much loved creatures (all of which are thorns that the earth produced after sin), come upon them [My servants], they endure them all with the light of reason and holy faith, looking to Me, who am the Supreme Good, and who cannot desire other than good, for which I permit these tribulations through love, and not through hatred.[99]

Charity exerts a second influence upon faith which, although included after a fashion in the preceding, is nevertheless distinct from it and peculiar to faith. Faith is a virtue which inclines us to give absolute credence to the divine teachings although our mind does not perceive their intrinsic truth. When it is a question of living faith, our mind yields this belief to the word of God under the impulse of charity. The more charity we have, therefore, the more solid and vital is our belief. St. Catherine is thinking of this altogether special action of charity upon faith, for example, when she writes these words quoted above: "Know that it is love which makes us believers. We have faith in what we love;" or again in a letter to Monna Lodovica di Granello: "This sweet charity carries with it the light of most holy faith which, under the influence of the love it bears for its Creator, truly believes that God desires nothing

---

[98] Letter T31.

[99] *Dialogue*, chapter 45.

but its welfare.[100] Charity not only stabilizes belief, but increases the very light of faith. To the papal legate in Tuscany, the Benedictine monk Gerard du Puy, St. Catherine writes:

> The furnace of charity produces in the soul the same effects as a material fire. It warms, enlightens, transforms all into fire.... The soul is illumined by it so that there is no longer any darkness remaining in it. Thus enlightened by his holy flame, it opens wide the door of its understanding and dilates it.[101]

⇧

Much more characteristic, however, are St. Catherine's observations regarding the action of faith on charity. Again, we see asserting itself in her the peculiar spirit of her religious family.

> He who know more [it is God who speaks] loves Me more, and he who loves Me more receives more. Your reward is measured according to the measure of your love, and if you should ask Me, whether one who has no knowledge [such as faith gives] can attain to this love, I should reply, yes it is possible that he may attain to it, but an individual case does not make a general law and I always discourse to you in general.[102]

The *Dialogue* explains to us, moreover, in detail this fostering action of faith with regard to charity:

> A man in mortal sin is deprived of the life of grace [which is living faith], and he who is in grace has illuminated the eye of his intellect to know Me, who gave him both grace and the virtue which preserves it, and, in that light, he knows the misery and the reason of sin, that is to say, his own self-love, on which account he hates it, and thereby receives the warmth of Divine love into his affection, which follows his intellect.... For, as soon as the eye of the intellect lifts itself with the pupil of

---

[100] Letter T304.

[101] Letter T109.

[102] *Dialogue*, chapter 131,

faith above sensual vision in the contemplation of Me, affection follows it, loving that which the intellect sees and knows.[103]

The whole mystery of the relations between faith and charity is clarified in the following celebrated passage from the *Dialogue*:

> The soul I created in My image and likeness, giving her memory, intellect, and will. The intellect is the most noble part of the soul, and is moved by the affection, and nourishes it....The soul cannot live without love, but always wants to love something, because she is made of love, and, by love, I created her. And therefore I told you that the affection moved the intellect [and charity moves faith in a soul in the state of grace], saying, as it were, *"I will love, because the food on which I feed is love."* Then the intellect [with faith], feeling itself awakened by the affection, says, as it were, "If you will love, I will give you that which you can love." And at once it arises, considering carefully the dignity of the soul, and the indignity into which she has fallen through sin. In the dignity of her being it tastes My inestimable goodness, and the uncreated charity with which I created her, and, in contemplating her misery, it discovers and tastes My mercy, and sees how, through mercy, I have lent her time and drawn her out of darkness. Then the affection nourishes itself in love.[104]

Occasionally, St. Catherine condenses this admirable doctrine into concise and daring formulae: "Love is measured by faith and faith by love."[105] Or again: "With this light the souls in the unitive state love Me, because loves follows the intellect, and the more it knows the more it can love. Thus the one feeds the other."[106] *L'amore va dietro all'intelletto* [love follows the intellect]; that is the statement which best characterizes this entire teaching which is so thoroughly Dominican.

---

[103] *Dialogue*, chapter 119.

[104] *Dialogue*, chapter 51.

[105] Letter to Friar Raymond of Capua; T344.

[106] *Dialogue*, chapter 85.

⚜

Finally, by way of conclusion, a simple observation regarding the object of faith. To bring to light the favorite viewpoint and spirit of St. Catherine it will suffice to present the beautiful words which are to be found reiterated in twenty different contexts of the *Dialogue* and the Letters:

> But understand that all this cannot be learned without light and without the book. The eye of the intellect must therefore be illumined by the light of most holy faith and the book must be written wherein we read this teaching. Now if I see things correctly, very dear brother, God has given us the eye of the intellect and, in that eye, the light of faith.... He has likewise given us the book. That book is written upon the word of the cross, not with ink, but with blood. Its illuminated capitals are the most sweet and holy wounds of Christ. Can anyone be so ignorant and so uncouth, so lacking in comprehension as not to be able to read it?[107]

Such, in brief and in orderly arrangement, is the beautiful teaching of St. Catherine regarding the virtue of faith the eulogy of which forms the conclusion of her *Dialogue*.[108]

IX. The Three Lights

This teaching on the three lights is found in two places among the writings of St. Catherine: in chapters 97-100 of the *Dialogue* and in a letter to the Augustinian hermit, Friar William Flete, the Englishman.[109]

In the *Dialogue* this teaching is introduced by way of a question Catherine poses to her divine Master. She asks Him to enlighten her regarding a doubt:

---

[107] Letter to Jean of Parma; T309.

[108] *Dialogue*, chapter 167.

[109] Letter T64; Scudder, p. 60.

When a person desirous of serving You, comes to me, or to some other servant of yours to ask for counsel, how should I teach him? I know, sweet and Eternal God, that You did reply to this question—"I am He who takes delight in few words and many deeds." Nevertheless, if it please Your goodness to grant me a few words on the subject, it will cause me the greatest pleasure. And also, if on some occasion, when I am praying for Your creatures, and in particular for Your servants, and I seem to see the subjects of my prayer, in one I find (in the course of my prayer) a well-disposed mind, a soul rejoicing in You; and in another, as it might seem to me, a mind full of darkness; have I the right, O Eternal Father, to judge the one soul to be in light, and the other in darkness? Or, supposing I should see that the one lives in great penance, and the other does not, should I be right to judge that he who does the greater penance has the higher perfection? I pray You, so that I may not be deceived through my limited vision, that You would declare to me in detail, what You have already said in general on this matter.[110]

Such is the doubt St. Catherine begs God to resolve for her. It is a complex one, dealing more particularly with the value of facility, taste for, and consolation in prayer and practices of penance, as signs of perfection. Fr. Hurtaud[111] rightly observes that this question has reference to the teaching previously received by Catherine on the virtue of discretion or supernatural prudence.[112] Nevertheless it must be considered that, if she is anxious about this point, it is in terms of a doctrine of perfection to be transmitted to souls of good will and with which she asks God, once more, to deign to gratify her.

Let us gather up the new lights which God gives to Catherine on this virtue which, good Thomist that she is, she esteems so highly.

In order that you may the better understand what I shall say to you, I shall revert to the beginning of your request concerning the three lights which issue from Me, the True Light. The first is a general light dwelling in those who live in ordinary charity....

---

[110] *Dialogue*, chapter 97.

[111] Ibid.

[112] Cf. Chapter V.

The other two lights dwell in those who, having abandoned the world, desire perfection.[113]

But now the exposition becomes complicated in a somewhat surprising way:

> You know, as I have told you, that, without the light, no one can walk in the truth, that is, without the light of reason, which light of reason you draw from Me the True Light, by means of the eye of your intellect and the light of faith which I have given you in holy baptism.... For, in baptism, and through the mediation of the Blood of My only-begotten Son, you have received the form of faith; which faith you exercise in virtue by the light of reason, which gives you life and causes you to walk in the path of truth, and, by its means [faith], to arrive at Me, the True Light, for, without it, you would plunge into darkness.[114]

In this light, common to all those who are in charity, it is impossible not to recognize the light of the theological virtue of faith which we have already studied.[115] But it is a light which is taken for granted here and not included among the three lights with which we are now concerned. God the Father continues, in fact: "It is necessary for you to have two lights derived from this primary light, and to these I will also add a third." This is an involved formulae but is clarified by what follows: In a certain sense, there are only two lights, an imperfect light and a perfect light, but the latter is twofold, which results finally in three. In the letter to William Flete, St. Catherine says that there are two lights, the imperfect and the perfect, but "two kinds of perfect people walk in this perfect light," which amounts to the same thing.

"Two lights," we are told, "derived from this primary light...." But what light? The true Light which is God himself? Or the primary light of faith? It is not made clear. However it would seem to be the light of faith which, moreover, combines with that of reason to form the total light of Christian reason, of sacred doctrine, of holy theology. Once more we

---

[113] *Dialogue*, chapter 98.

[114] Ibid.

[115] Chapter VIII.

have the impression of finding ourselves on the familiar ground of Thomistic thought. Let us now enter into the very quick of our subject:

> The first [light] lightens you all to know the transitory nature of the things of the world, all of which pass like wind. But this you cannot know thoroughly, unless you first recognize your own fragility, how strong is your inclination, through the law of perversity with which your members are bound, to rebel[116] against Me, your Creator.

The eternal Father is not reluctant to admit, moreover, that it is He who has imposed this law, and He explains his reasons which are two in number.

> (Not that by this law any man can be constrained to commit any, even the smallest sin, against his will, but that this law of perversity fights lustily against the spirit). I did not impose this law upon you, in order that My rational creature should be conquered by it, but in order that he should prove and increase the virtue of his soul, because virtue cannot be proved, except by its contrary. Sensuality is contrary to the spirit, and yet, by means of sensuality, the soul is able to prove the love which she has for Me, her Creator. How does she prove it? When, with anger and displeasure, she rises against herself. This law has also been imposed in order to preserve the soul in true humility. Wherefore you see that, while, I created the soul to my own image and likeness, placing her in such dignity and beauty, I caused her to be accompanied by the vilest of all things, imposing on her the law of perversity, imprisoning her in a body, formed of the vilest substance of the earth, so that, seeing in what her true beauty consisted, she should not raise her head in pride against Me. Wherefore, to one who possess this light, the fragility of his body is a cause of humiliation to the soul, and is in no way matter for pride, but rather for true and perfect humility. So that this law does not constrain you to any sin by its strivings, but supplies a reason to make you know yourselves and the instability of the world. This should be seen

---

[116] *Dialogue*, chapter 98.

by the eye of the intellect, with light of the holy faith, of which I said to you that it was the pupil of the eye.[117]

Thus we find ourselves brought back to our light, the first of the three. But there is an unexpected complication: God describes this light in terms which seem to identify it with the very light of the virtue of faith. We can no longer follow, convinced as we were that the virtue of faith represented a preliminary light, a kind of focal point whence radiated all three lights, distinct and new. On the other hand, it is difficult not to think, while reading what has gone before, of that characteristic, primordial element in all spiritual life which St. Catherine calls self-knowledge. From all appearances, the knowledge of self in God is the fruit of the first of these three lights with which we are dealing. But may we really believe that it represents an action of the theological virtue of faith itself? Let us read further:

This is that light which is necessary in general to every rational creature, whatever may be his condition, who wishes to participate in the life of grace, in the fruit of the Blood of the immaculate Lamb. This is the ordinary light, that is, the light which all persons must possess, as has been said, for, without it, the soul would be in a state of damnation. And, for this reason, because the soul, being without the light, is not in a state of grace, inasmuch as, not having the light, she does not know the evil of her sin or its cause, and therefore cannot avoid or hate it. And similarly if the soul knows not good, and the reason of good, that is to say virtue, she cannot love or desire either Me, who am the Essential Good, or virtue, which I have given you as an instrument and means for you to receive My grace, and myself the True Good. See then how necessary is this light, for your sins consist in nothing else than in loving that which I hate, and in hating that which I love. I love virtue and hate vice; he who loves vice and hates virtue offends Me, and is deprived of My grace. Such a one walks as if blind, for he knows not the cause of vice, that is, his sensual self-love, nor does he hate himself on account of it; he is ignorant of vice and of the evil which follows it; he is ignorant of virtue and of Me, who am the cause of his obtaining life giving virtue; he is ignorant of his

---

[117] Ibid.

own dignity, which he should maintain by advancing to grace, by means of virtue. See, therefore, how this ignorance is the cause of all this evil, and how you also need this light, as has been said.[118]

When all is said and done, we have only one detail by which to identify this first light, namely what it enables us to discover. But this detail strengthens our conviction, everything considered, that it belongs to the virtue of discretion or supernatural prudence rather than to the theological virtue of faith, providing however that we do not forget the close relationship existing between prudence and faith vivified by charity, and admit that, for St. Catherine as well as for St. Thomas Aquinas, the light of supernatural prudence or discretion is only the extension, the radiation of the light of faith in the sphere of moral action.

⇧

In contrast to this first imperfect light which is necessary and common to all those in the state of grace, there is a perfect light. The relationship between the two is difficult to determine precisely.

> When the soul has arrived at the attainment of the general light, of which I have spoken, she should not remain contented, because, as long as you are pilgrims in this life, you are capable of growth, and he who does not go forward, by that very fact, is turning back. She should either grow in the general light, which she has acquired through My grace, or anxiously strive to attain to the second and perfect light, leaving the imperfect and reaching the perfect. For, if the soul truly has light, she will wish to arrive at perfection.[119]

Between the ordinary light acquired with the help of grace wherein one may continue to progress, and this perfect light, must there be then, as it were, a difference of nature or of order, the former pertaining to the order of the virtues and the latter to the order of the gifts, or as we should say today, to the mystical order? Adopting this latter hypothesis, we should have to admit that, for St. Catherine, the so-called mystical ways are accessible to every soul in the state of grace who earnestly

---

[118] Ibid.

[119] *Dialogue*, chapter 99.

strives to enter upon them. In her letter to William Flete she declares simply: "The soul must not stay content because it has arrived at gaining the general light; no, it ought to go on with all zeal to the perfect light. For, since men are at first imperfect rather than perfect, they should advance in light to perfection." There is no longer any question of progress proper to the imperfect light.

But let us see what this perfect light is. "In this second perfect light are to be found two kinds of perfection; for they may be called perfect who have abandoned the general way of living in the world" [of imperfect Christians, we surmise].[120] The distinction is manifestly drawn between the perfect and not between the lights themselves. The same is true in the letter to William Flete. Nonetheless, this division has a bearing upon the light since it really determines the distinction between the perfect.

Regarding the first kind of perfect souls and this second light wherein they live, we read as follows:

> In this second perfect light are to be found two kinds of perfection.... One perfection is that of those who give themselves up wholly to the castigation of the body, doing great and severe penance. These, in order that their sensuality may not rebel against their reason, have placed their desire rather in the mortification of the body than in the destruction of their self-will, as I have explained to you in another place. These feed their souls at the table of penance, and are good and perfect, if their penance be illuminated by discretion, and founded on Me, if, that is to say, they act with true knowledge of themselves and of Me [which we can clearly see here as pertaining to discretion], with great humility, and wholly conformed to the judgment of My will, and not to that of the will of man. But, if they were not thus clothed with My will, in true humility, they would often offend against their own perfection, esteeming themselves the judges of those who do not walk in the same path. Do you know why this would happen to them? Because they have placed all their labor and desire in the mortification of the body, rather than in the destruction of their own will. Such as these wish always to choose their own times, and

---

120 Ibid.

places, and consolations, after their own fashion, and also the persecutions of the world and of the Devil, as I have narrated to you in speaking of the second state of perfection. They say, cheating themselves with the delusion of their own self-will, which I have already called their spiritual self-will, "I wish to have that consolation, and not these battles, or these temptations of the Devil, not, indeed, for my own pleasure, but in order to please God the more, and in order to retain Him the more in my soul through grace; because it seems to me that I should possess Him more, and serve Him better in that way than in this." And this is the way the soul often falls into trouble, and becomes tedious and insupportable to herself, thus injuring her own perfection; yet she does not perceive it, nor that, within her, lurks the stench of pride, and there she lies. Now, if the soul were not in this condition, but were truly humble and not presumptuous, she would be illuminated to see that I, the Primary and sweet Truth, grant condition, and time, and place, and consolations, and tribulations as they may be needed for your salvation, and to complete the perfection to which I have elected the soul. And she would see that I give everything through love, and that therefore, with love and reverence, should she receive everything.[121]

This second light, like the first, is described to us less in its essence than in its effects. It is nonetheless evident that it is a practical light, a light of discretion, that is to say, of supernatural prudence. But the close connection still stands out between discretion and faith, between the light which enlightens us as to the choice of means and the primordial light which reveals to us the very objectives of our spiritual light, establishing us in present contemplation of them. It is a beautiful trait of both St. Catherine's and St. Thomas' teaching, replete with the direct, loving gaze upon God, which makes it so dominating in its basic inspiration yet so flexible in its practical application, so intelligent in its unity, so ardent and so humble. The problem of discovering whether this discretion, qualified as perfect although still containing an admixture of imperfection, belongs to the order of the infused virtue of prudence alone, or proceeds from the gifts, that is to say, particularly from the gift of counsel—this problem seems to hold little interest for St. Catherine.

---

[121] Ibid.

She seems very far from admitting into supernatural life that very pronounced, somewhat material dualism distinguishing ordinary spiritual life from so-called mystical life, which seems to satisfy some minds. The life of grace is all one for her as it is for St. Thomas, the common work of the virtues and gifts. This is more or less true in every state of the supernatural life, even the imperfect. In the more perfect states, it is still the virtues which play the principal role since the gifts themselves are exercised in connection with them and for their benefit. Furthermore, what is true of the gifts is also true of the gratuitous graces whose frequent existence and importance in the so-called mystical states must be recognized. The supernatural life is fundamentally the work of the infused virtues and principally of the theological virtues with which the gifts are interdependent and to which they are in a certain way subordinate.

From the place where we paused in the *Dialogue*, St. Catherine, still transcribing the divine teachings in her direct style, continues in the following terms:

> Those who belong to the third state, which immediately follows the last, having arrived at this glorious light, are perfect in every condition in which they may be, and receive every event which I permit to happen to them with due reverence.... They deem themselves worthy of the troubles and stumbling-blocks caused them by the world, and of the privation of their own consolation, and indeed of whatever circumstance happens to them. And inasmuch as they deem themselves worthy of trouble, so also do they deem themselves unworthy of the fruit which they receive after their trouble. They have known and tasted in the light My Eternal Will, which wishes naught else but your good, and gives and permits these troubles in order that you should be sanctified in Me. [This important corrective should be remarked: the perfect soul can renounce all personal care for her own good because she is aware that God concerns Himself with her. And she makes this divine will her own in the very act by which she surrenders her own will.] Wherefore the soul having known My Will, clothes herself with it, and fixes her attention on nothing else except seeing in what way she can preserve and increase her perfection to the glory and praise of My Name, opening the eye of her intellect and fixing it in the light of faith upon Christ crucified, My only-begotten Son, loving

and following His doctrine, which is the rule of the road for perfect and imperfect alike.... When therefore the soul has arrived at seeing, knowing, and tasting, in its full sweetness, this light, she runs, as one enamored and inflamed with love, to the table of holy desire; she does not see herself in herself, seeking her own consolation either spiritual or temporal, but, like one who has placed his all in this light and knowledge, and has destroyed his own will, she shuns no labor from whatever source it comes, but rather enduring the troubles, the insults, the temptations of the Devil, and the murmurings of men, eats at the table of the most holy Cross, the food of the honor of Me, the Eternal God, and of the salvation of souls; seeking no reward, either from Me or from creatures, because she is stripped of mercenary love, that is of love for Me based on interested motives, and is clothed in perfect light, loving Me in perfect purity, with no other regard than for the praise and glory of My Name, serving neither Me for her own delight, nor her neighbor for her own profit, but purely through love alone.[122]

It is sufficiently evident that this is St. Catherine's own way, manifestly inherited from St. Dominic.

Contrasting this light and this way still more directly with that which preceded it, St. Catherine continues:

Such as these have lost themselves, and have stripped themselves of the old man, that is of their own sensuality, and, having clothed themselves with the New Man, the sweet Christ Jesus, my Truth, follow Him manfully. These are they who sit at the table of holy desire, having been more anxious to slay their own will than to slay and mortify their own body. They have indeed mortified their body, though not as an end in itself, but as a means which helps them to stay their own will...and so ought you to do.[123]

---

[122] *Dialogue*, chapters 99 and 100.

[123] *Dialogue*, chapter 100.

The subject is then developed in terms and in a spirit which is altogether plausible and deserving of all our attention:

> Their principal desire should be to slay their own will, so that it may not seek or wish anything else than to follow my sweet Truth, Christ crucified, seeking the honor and glory of My name and the salvation of souls. Those who are in this sweet light know it, and remain constantly in peace and quiet, and no one scandalizes them, for they have cut away that thing by which stumbling-blocks are caused, namely their own will. And all the persecutions, with which the world and the Devil can attack them, slide under their feet, standing, as they do, in the waters of many tribulations and temptations, and do not hurt them, for they remain attached to Me by the umbilical cord of fiery desire. Such a man rejoices in everything, nor does he make himself judge of My servants, or of any rational creature, but rejoices in every condition and in every manner of holiness which he sees, saying: "Thanks be to You, Eternal Father, who have in Your House many mansions." And he rejoices more in the different ways of holiness which he sees, than if he were to see all traveling by one road, because, in this way, he perceives the greatness of My goodness become more manifest, and thus, rejoicing, draws from all the fragrance of the rose. And not only in the case of good, but even when he sees something evidently sinful, he does not fall into judgment, but rather into true and holy compassion, interceding with Me for sinners and saying, with perfect humility: "Today it is your turn, and tomorrow it will be mine unless the divine grace preserve me."[124]

But we should complete the description:

> These [whose love is ordered in Me] do not lose their time in passing false judgments, either on My servants or the servants of the world, and they are never scandalized by any murmurings of men, either for their own sake or that of others. That is to say, in their own case they are content to endure anything for My name's sake; and when an injury is done to some one else, they endure it with compassion of this injured

---

124 Ibid.

neighbor, and without murmuring against him who caused the injury, or him who received it.[125]

All of this conjures up the ardent soul of St. Catherine and her vocation.

Such are the three lights, lights of discretion and of prudence, but under and within the higher light of faith.

---

[125] Ibid.

Lemonnyer
Appendix A

A part of these studies by the late Fr. Lemonnyer on the spirituality of St. Catherine of Siena was published by *L'Annee Dominicaine*; the rest is unpublished. Taken together they form two parts. The first, written earlier and consisting of the more considerable portion, presents the general outline of our interior growth according to St. Catherine; the second defines the role played in this interior growth by faith and the ever more vivid illuminations of the virtue of prudence. In gathering them together into one volume we have considered not only our devotion to St. Catherine, whom every Friar Preacher loves as his mother, and our gratitude toward one of our best teachers, but their own intrinsic value. St. Catherine is an incomparable teacher of sanctity. She possesses a precise sense of the humblest realities of human life, a perfect sureness of doctrine, an experiential knowledge of the highest mystical ways. But to understand her teachings an initiation is necessary. Fr. Lemonnyer gives it to us. A solid theologian, a keen psychologist, a loving, attentive disciple,[1] he penetrated into the most delicate nuances of her thought, and he brings into clear relief its essential lines for our benefit. Let us add what gives his work an added charm: he knows how to translate her delightful Tuscan idiom into a French that is full of flavor. Thus, under its modest appearance, this little volume contains a luminous treatise, attractive and devoid of banality, on the most sublime spiritual theology. It may be summarized as follows.

Our spiritual life ought to proceed from the *knowledge of ourselves in God*, that is to say, from the consciousness of our misery and our greatness, from the consideration of God's mercy and bounty toward us.[2] We acquire this knowledge by the light of reason and faith which are

---

[1] At the time of his death, in 1932, Lemonnyer was preparing a life of St. Catherine of Siena for the French collection, *Les Saints*.

[2] See the First and Second Parts of this work.

mutually interdependent.[3] From the conviction that we are nothing, *humility* is born in us, impelling us to self-abasement, as God abased himself in Jesus Christ.[4] Progress in the knowledge of ourselves in God and the cultivation of humility secures in us the growth of divine *charity.* This is the true life of our soul which alone unites us to God.[5] From charity proceeds *discernment* or supernatural prudence, giving us a just appreciation of all our duties;[6] the more highly developed this discernment becomes, the more it commits us to the way of perfection, until it causes us to renounce completely our self-will.[7] From charity is derived *patience,* the enlightened, loving endurance of the trials of life.[8] From charity is born *fortitude*, ensuring the supremacy of our free will over sensibility.[9] Finally, from charity there issues forth an admirable flowering of all the moral virtues together with a passionate zeal for the honor of God and the salvation of all men and women.[10]

Thus does Fr. Lemonnyer become our guide and we may trust ourselves to his wisdom. His analyses must be read slowly and pondered well; a hasty perusal would grasp neither their solidity nor their richness. Since he very often quotes Catherine herself, we have indicated the references to all these passages; it will not be difficult, then, to have recourse to them. In the *Dialogue*, we have given the number of the chapter; for the *Letters*, whose classification varies with the different editors, we have adhered to the edition of Gigli (1713), the French translation by Cartier (1858), and Tommaseo's edition (1860).[11] In union with Fr. Lemonnyer himself, we hope this little volume, by facilitating the study of St. Catherine directly and in person, will increase the

---

[3] Chapter VIII.

[4] Chapter III.

[5] Chapter IV.

[6] Chapter V.

[7] Chapter IX.

[8] Chapter VI.

[9] Chapter VII.

[10] Chapters I and IV.

[11] Reprinted through the good offices of Misciatelli (1913-1921). [Because the numbering of Catherine's letters by Tommaseo is now almost universally used, we will cite only this numbering system preceded by the letter T].

number of those who draw inspiration from her beneficent teaching for the conduct of their souls.

Joseph Perinelle, O.P.

Lemonnyer
Appendix B

Table of Contents

Made in the USA
Middletown, DE
02 May 2017